A
THIRST
FOR GOD

*Reflections on the
Forty-second and Forty-third
Psalms*

SHERWOOD ELIOT WIRT

Illustrations by Nancy Munger

ZONDERVAN PUBLISHING HOUSE
OF THE ZONDERVAN CORPORATION
GRAND RAPIDS, MICHIGAN 49506

To Harry and Evelyn

A THIRST FOR GOD
Copyright © 1980 by Sherwood Eliot Wirt

Unless otherwise indicated, quotations of Scripture are from *The Holy Bible, The New International Version*, copyright © 1978 by the New York International Bible Society. Used by permission. The author prefers variant readings for portions of Psalms 42 and 43, indicated in the text by the use of italics.

Library of Congress Cataloging in Publication Data

Wirt, Sherwood Eliot.
  A thirst for God.

    1. Bible. O.T. Psalms XLII—Meditations. 2. Bible. O.T. Psalms XLIII—Meditations. I. Title.
BS 1450 42d.W57   223'.206   80-12361
ISBN 0-310-34640-1

Printed in the United States of America

Contents

Acknowledgments

My appreciation goes to the following persons for their generous help during the preparation of this book:

Mrs. Kay Gudnason of Moraga, California, who made available her extensive personal library on the Psalms.

The librarians at San Diego State University, the University of San Diego, Point Loma College, Christian Heritage College, the San Diego County Library, and the *San Diego Union*, who provided invaluable assistance.

Dr. Robert K. DeVries, Mr. Fritz Ridenour, and Mr. James E. Ruark of Zondervan Publishing House, who not only read the manuscript, but improved it greatly. I cannot thank them enough.

Members of the Christian Writers' Guild of San Diego County, who listened to the text and whose critiques never failed to amend it.

Rev. Chuck Smith and Rev. Armin Gesswein, who read portions of the manuscript.

The editors of *Decision* magazine, who granted permission to quote from six articles published during 1960–76, when I was editor.

Miss Violet M. Dunbar of Charlotte, North Carolina, who prepared the typescript after much retyping and "counted it all joy."

My wife, Winola Wells Wirt, and our son, Alexander Wells Wirt, who provided counsel and encouragement.

Besides these, many others have influenced and shaped my thinking. To all I say, God bless you and thank you.

S.E.W.

Poway, California
January 1980

Psalms 42 and 43

For the director of music.
A *maskil* of the Sons of Korah.

As the deer pants for streams of water,   *1*
   so my soul pants for you, O God.
My soul thirsts for God, for the living God.   *2*
   When can I go and meet with God?
My tears have been my   *3*
   food day and night,
while men say to me all day long,
   "Where is your God?"
These things I remember   *4*
   as I pour out my soul:
how I used to go with the multitude,
   leading the procession to the house of God,
with shouts of joy and thanksgiving
   among the festive throng.

Why are you downcast, O my soul?   *5*
   Why so disturbed within me?
Put your hope in God,
   for I will yet praise him
   for the salvation of his face.
O my God, my soul is downcast within me;   *6*
   therefore I will remember you
from the land of the Jordan,
   the heights of Hermon—from Mount Mizar.
Deep calls to deep   *7*
   in the roar of your waterfalls;
all your waves and breakers
   have swept over me.

By day the Lord directs his love,   *8*
   at night his song is with me—
   a prayer to the God of my life.

I say to God my Rock, 9
   "Why have you forgotten me?
Why must I go about mourning,
   oppressed by the enemy?"
My bones suffer mortal agony 10
   as my foes taunt me,
saying to me all day long,
   "Where is your God?"

Why are you downcast, O my soul? 11
   Why so disturbed within me?
Put your hope in God,
   for I will yet praise him,
   the salvation of my face and my God.

Vindicate me, O God, 1
   and plead my cause against an ungodly nation;
   rescue me from deceitful and wicked men.
You are God my *Fortress*. 2
   Why have you rejected me?
Why must I go about mourning,
   oppressed by the enemy?
Send forth your light and your truth, 3
   let them guide me;
let them bring me to your holy mountain,
   to the place where you dwell.
Then will I go to the altar of God, 4
   to God, my joy and my delight.
I will praise you with the harp,
   O God, my God.

Why are you downcast, O my soul? 5
   Why so disturbed within me?
Put your hope in God,
   for I will yet praise him,
   the salvation of my face and my God.

CHAPTER ONE

On the Run

As the deer pants for streams of water,
so my soul pants for you, O God.
—Psalm 42:1

THE THIRSTY DEER

Trout are playing in the quiet eddy of a mountain stream. A hawk flaps its way to the top of a giant pine. Out of the creek willow growth emerges a deer, exhausted, its flanks heaving. In the distance a rifle cracks. The deer freezes an instant, then stalks warily to the water's edge and bends its neck to drink.

So, if we add an imaginative touch, our Psalm might be said to begin. But as I leaf through a stack of standard commentaries, I come across a different kind of imagination. One scholar thinks the deer is a stag, another a doe. One says the deer is panting because dogs have been chasing it; another says no, it is a victim of seasonal drouth. Still another quotes Appian and other ancient zoologists as saying that deer become thirsty because they eat snakes—"whose poison, diffused through their entrails, produces a burning heat and fever."[1]

Beloved, I am not about to sink you into a quagmire of scholastic trivia. Like you, I am thirsty for God. I intend to walk with you through the Forty-second and Forty-third Psalms in the hope that the Holy Spirit will use these well-marked pathways to lead us into his truth.

Most of us have been chased by dogs—that is, we have been pressured and hounded by all manner of forces until we think being short of breath is normal. As for spiritual drouth, it gets to the best of us. So whatever the interpreters decide, we can identify with the deer.

So far as I can discover, mine is only the second book to appear in English on the Forty-second Psalm, the first being published in 1863 under the title *The Hart and the Waterbrooks: a Practical Exposition*, by one Reverend John R. MacDuff. Parenthetically I had thought of calling this book *An Impractical Exposition*, for reasons which will doubtless soon become apparent.

But I don't consider that I—or Mr. MacDuff, for that matter—need to apologize for making a portion of the Psalter the vehicle of our thinking. Nothing in the history of world literature can compare with the eloquence of the Psalms. Millions of people who have learned them by heart will testify to their genius and power. Dean A. F. Kirkpatrick describes them as "the outpouring of the heart to God in the most intimate personal communion . . . springing out of the needs and aspirations of the soul in the crises of life."[2]

There is a preparation of the heart in these glorious songs, and Christianity would be unthinkable without them. No part of the Bible is more universally loved. In types and figures the essence of the Gospel is here for those who have eyes to see, even though the Psalms were written and sung hundreds of years before Christ.

As for the Forty-second and Forty-third Psalms themselves, their continuing popularity through the centuries at-
tests to their value. Apart from the help they have given to
millions, they contain some of the most superb lyric poetry
ever written. "Whoever wrote them," says Alexander Maclaren, "gave immortal form to the longings of the soul after
God."[3] But if they are timeless, they are also timely; we shall
see that they express a good bit of the modern mood.

As we move through these two Psalms that open the second
book of the Psalter, we may find God speaking directly to us.
The purpose of our Bible study is not merely to absorb information, but to get from where we are to where we want to go.
Not to let the deer pant until its heart bursts, but to get it to
the streams of water. We will find that our two Psalms cut
through a lot of religious underbrush. They isolate the basic
issues. They indicate the direction we should take. If we are
willing to face the facts and listen to the Spirit as he ministers
to us through the Word, who knows what might happen to us?

Jesus understood the problem of the human thirst for God
himself. At the Feast of Tabernacles in Jerusalem he said, "If a
man is thirsty, let him come to me and drink."[4] I believe with
all my heart that Jesus slakes the thirst for God expressed in
these Psalms. In his life and teaching Jesus does not supplant
the Psalms; he fulfills them. When we receive him as our
Savior and are given the right to become sons and daughters
of God, we are joined, not to a cause or to a body of literature,
but to a Person—Jesus himself.

In today's apocalyptic mood the thirst for God has been
overshadowed by Bible studies that seem to be more exciting.
Much attention is being devoted to prophecy. Instead of
seeking God's presence in their lives, many are simply
speculating as to what God will do next. But there is only so
much room for speculation.

Consider, for example, the well-known prophecy of the Old
Testament prophet Joel. A time would come, he said, when
God would "pour out my Spirit on all people."[5] The apostle
Peter, centuries later, declared to those who had gathered in
Jerusalem for the Feast of Pentecost that Joel's prophecy was

being fulfilled in their presence.[6] Yet many Bible students say Joel's prophecy also points to a future time when world-wide revival will take place. I like to think they are right. Before the final judgment, the Holy Spirit will be poured out upon all nations, and the deep human thirst will be quenched as men and women see the presence and power of God in a mighty awakening. What a glorious prospect! What a baring of God's arm! But how can we know if or when it will come? We simply do not have the information.

But we do have the Psalms. They can prepare us for revival in our own hearts. Then if God sends a gracious outpouring of his Spirit into the church, we will be ready.

Our Lord said, "Blessed are those who hunger and thirst for righteousness, for they will be filled."[7] If we are thirsty deer, that is a good sign. Whatever tomorrow brings, we need water from the Fountain today.

THE VOICE

Every human being would like to be more than he is. That is what makes him a human being. Dogs are content with their dogginess and sheep with their sheepishness, but not people. Whatever you may think about the question of origins, animals and humans can be said to have this difference: animals as a rule are satisfied to be what they are, humans are not.

What is this discontent that keeps us bipeds struggling for something beyond what we are? What I am describing goes deeper than cravings of the flesh. Some call it the "human spirit." But what is this spirit? Is it angelic or demonic? When we look to Scripture we read, "The spirit of man is the candle of the Lord."[8] Yes, that makes sense. A candle is only a piece of beeswax until it is lit: well-tooled, highly processed, most significant beeswax no doubt—but still beeswax. So we learn from the proverb that the human spirit, for all its yearning, remains unfulfilled until it is touched by the divine flame.

In the opening verse of the Forty-second Psalm we find even clearer imagery. Picturing a spent deer in an exhausting, dehydrating situation, the Psalmist says, "That's where I am. I

am the deer." What is his problem? It is the perennial problem of the unsatisfied human spirit in its thirst for God. The
Psalmist is driven by the pursuit of God, goaded by the longing for God, and he will be satisfied by nothing less than a
direct confrontation with the Almighty. To settle for some
delegated authority is unthinkable. He wants God himself.

We ought to note that this questing motif is not found in all
the Psalms. The well-known Twenty-third, in particular,
sounds as if the Psalmist's struggle is over: "I shall not want.
He makes me to lie down in green pastures . . . beside still
waters."

So in Psalm 23 the deer has reached the water, but in Psalm
42 he is not there yet. The difference between the Psalms may
be explained partly by a difference in authorship. A strong
tradition links David, the shepherd-king, to the Twenty-third
Psalm as its author. But Psalms 42 and 43 belong to the second book of the five books of Psalms; and at the head of Psalm
42, both in Hebrew and in Greek (LXX), appear the words,
"For the director of music. A *maskil* of the Sons of Korah." No
one knows exactly what the word *maskil* means; but the
Korahites, we are told in 2 Chronicles 20:19, were renowned
in King Jehoshaphat's day as singers and musicians. They
were descended from Korah, who was involved in a rebellion
against Moses; but Korah's children were not affected by the
judgment that fell upon their father. Many commentators
consider that Psalms 42 and 43 are really one Psalm and were
among several Psalms composed by the Korahite family. "The
actual author, as one of a band of kinsmen who worked and
sang together . . . let his song go forth as one of the band."[9]

We need to identify this man if we can. We need to estab-
lish his credibility and make sure that his thirst for God is
genuine. If he could get beyond the religious routine of his
time, perhaps there is hope for us. "My soul pants for you, O
God!" To transcend the tight little orbit of our lives, to sit with
Mary at the feet of Jesus and glow in the rapture of divine
love—oh! for a taste of that, we say. And by saying it, we join
a great tradition.

In his *Confessions*, written about 400 A.D., Augustine cried out, "Who will give me what it takes to rest in you? Who will make it so you come into my heart and captivate it, so I can forget my rottenness and take hold of you, the one good thing in my life?"[10] A thousand years later Lady Julian of Norwich asked, "God, of your goodness give me yourself, for you are enough for me. If I ask anything less I know I shall continue to want. Only in you I have everything."[11]

The Puritan movement that shaped the character of North America was in the same tradition. We are familiar with the lampooning of the Puritan stereotype by essayists, historians, and cartoonists. Yet no one can study the great Puritan writers of three centuries ago without sensing that they were after more than proper behavior and social morality. Thomas Hooker, a Puritan preacher who, according to Perry Miller, "could put a king in his pocket," declared to the early settlers at Hartford, "The soul was made for an end, and good, and therefore for a better than it self, therefore for God, therefore to enjoy union with him, and communion with those blessed excellencies of his. . . ."[12]

Hooker would have rejected the human potential movement. He was not interested in self-actualization, self-realization, self-fulfillment, or self-satisfaction. Moonshots, health spas, and Bali Hai would have reaped his scorn along with the pursuit of happiness. His goals were not those of Epicurus or secular humanism. He wanted God.

Today it seems the Christian church is ready to cry out to God. But not for "union" with him—it hardly knows what that means. The church senses uneasily that it is being choked by its club life. It is drowning in decaffeinated coffee. It knows something is wrong, that there is more to life in the Spirit than what it has been getting. But it hasn't yet isolated the problem.

In January 1940, as I was contemplating studying for the ministry, an editorial appeared in *Fortune* magazine, of all places, which has haunted me ever since I read it. It said in part:

> So long as the church pretends or assumes to preach absolute
> values, but actually preaches relative and secondary values, it
> will merely hasten the process of disintegration. We are asked

to turn to the church for our enlightenment, but when we do so we find that the voice of the church is not inspired. The voice of the church today we find is the echo of our own voices. When we consult the church we hear only what we ourselves have said.

There is only one way out of the spiral and the way out is the sound of a voice, not our voice, but a voice coming from something beyond ourselves, in the existence of which we cannot disbelieve. It is the duty of the pastors to hear this voice, to cause us to hear it, and to tell us what it says.[13]

LORD, TEACH US

Where is the church either becoming or already weak? We could mention at random some of the British Commonwealth countries, western and northern Europe, and Japan. Where is it strong? In South Korea, parts of Indonesia, Poland, northeast India and India's Andhra state, parts of Africa south of the Sahara, the Solomon Islands, Tonga and Samoa—to list just a few places. What do we conclude? It would seem that superabundance and Spirit do not mix. What then can be said about America?

Look at this morning's mail: "Write to us. Join us. Sign here. Enroll there. Retreat with us. Advance with us. Buy this. Subscribe to that. Support this. Contribute to that. Take pity. View with alarm. Pick up the phone, call this number."

All advancing excellent causes, mind you. But that's just the trouble: God's causes have replaced God. So millions of Christians are asking, "Where are you, Lord? Are you in there somewhere, in all those thousands of electronic wires, in that cacophony of sound, in all that posted junk? Where are you? My soul is dry. Reading the Bible leaves me with a flat taste. I still believe, but the church bit has gone stale. I'm bored. I've heard everything, heard it until I'm sick of it. How can I cut across this dreary desert and find you?"

We might ask, too, why it is that so many of us seem to take our troubles into the pew on Sunday and bring them home again. We are quite aware that whatever it is our souls are doing, they are not panting after God. Yet we wish to be captivated. We wish in our hearts to be drunk with the wine of the Spirit. Blaise Pascal wrote,

There was once in man a true happiness, of which there now remains to him only an empty trace which he vainly tries to fill out of his environment. Yet all these efforts are inadequate, because the infinite abyss can only be filled by an infinite and immutable object, that is, by God himself.[14]

Veni, Creator Spiritus. We want to know the One who made us, and why he made us, and why he set us on this strange planet, and what he intends to do with us. We want to know if there is anything he can do with his church—or should we bypass it and let it go its antique way?

We know of course that there is more to Christian discipleship than falling on our faces before the altar. But many of us have never fallen on our faces before anything. We've just fallen, period. So we want to know how to get rid of the things that keep pushing us back and hindering us from following Jesus. And incidentally, how to swallow disappointment, and bear up under pain, and handle grief.

Martin Luther said that most Christians have enough religion to feel guilty about their sins, but not enough to enjoy life in the Spirit. Well, we are prepared to wrestle, if that is what it takes. We are ready to pant after God, but we really don't know how. Our souls are debilitated from lack of exercise. Lord, teach us to pant!

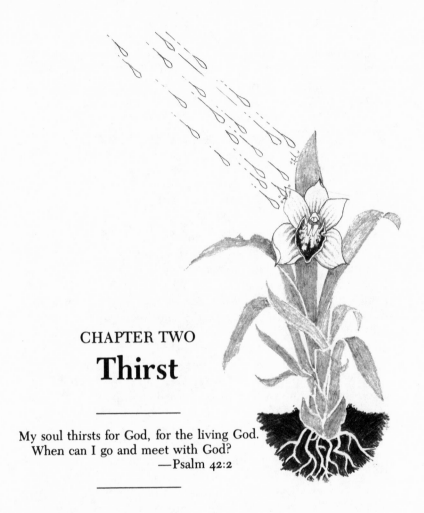

CHAPTER TWO
Thirst

My soul thirsts for God, for the living God.
When can I go and meet with God?
—Psalm 42:2

THE DRY RUN

The meaning of the Hebrew, scholars tell us, is "When may I come to appear in the presence of God?" They speculate that the Psalmist found himself in exile in the north; my guess is that he may have been held as a hostage. This much we know: in desiring to "meet with God" he longed to return to Jerusalem, where he could worship in the courts of the temple on Mount Zion.

But the Psalmist's desire is certainly more than simply a wish to get back to the sanctuary; as J. A. Motyer points out, "the yearning is for communication with God himself."[1] The feeling of this verse is reflected in the opening of Psalm 63, which is attributed to David:

> O God, you are my God,
> earnestly I seek you;
> my soul thirsts for you,
> my body longs for you,
> in a dry and weary land
> where there is no water.

Today millions of one-time churchgoers have reached the point where they not only avoid the sanctuary, but have lost all interest in God. He has become unreal to them. Were not the divine name so useful an expletive, many people would probably nominate God for oblivion and take a chance with their horoscopes. In view of God's continued popularity in the public opinion polls, however, those who have quit going to church prefer to maintain a safe distance. Like Voltaire, they would say of God, "We bow, but we do not speak."

Why do people feel that way? Why no thirst? What drove them away from church? Was it the worship service? Some services are more elaborate than others, but of the thousands of hours of worship conducted each week in Christian churches, I doubt if one is not sincere.

Armchair critics will single out particular faults to grumble about—the acoustics, the hard seats, the organist's hairstyle —but the exodus from the churches cannot be laid to such things. Buildings and personnel are only superficial causes. The churches are God's meeting houses, and when men and women no longer frequent them, it is because in some real way *the link between them and their Maker has been broken.*

What does it mean to thirst for the living God? Does it mean taking a vow, scaling the Matterhorn, fasting in the desert, meditating in a cave, swinging from a rope upside down over a fire, walking on coals, sleeping on spikes, cutting oneself in a frenzy, going unwashed, wearing uncomfortable clothing, doing things to one's hair, crawling, rolling, whirling, shaking, jumping for Jesus, or winning a ribbon for perfect Sunday school attendance?

All of these activities have been attempted, and more, in the name of religion; and it is not for me to condemn them. Isaiah the prophet walked stripped and barefoot for three years because God told him to.[2] But Isaiah was delivering a divine message to the people of Israel. His thirst had been met; he had already seen his Lord in the temple. Perhaps if you and I listen to some people whose love for God is beyond challenge, and who know how to express it, we shall find help in resolving this mystery. The glass through which we look will still be dark compared with the radiance of heaven; but at least it will not be opaque.

WE LISTEN

I propose to launch our quest-for-the-divine by tuning in on some of the great Christian voices of the past. These men and women may help us understand what the Psalmist's search was all about, and what he meant by "thirst." But lest we imagine that Jews and Christians have been the only ones ever to seek the face of God, listen first to this ancient Muslim prayer:

> O my Lord! If I worship you from fear of hell, burn me in hell; and if I worship you from hope of Paradise, exclude me from it; but if I worship you for your own sake, then withhold not from me your eternal Beauty.[3]

Now turn with me to my favorite teacher, Augustine.

> I came to love you late, O Beauty so ancient and so new; I came to love you late. You were within me and I was outside, where I rushed about wildly searching for you like some monster loose in your beautiful world. You were with me but I was not with you. You called me, you shouted to me, you broke past my deafness. You bathed me in your light, you wrapped me in your splendor, you sent my blindness reeling. You gave out such a delightful fragrance, and I drew it in and came breathing hard after you. I tasted, and it made me hunger and thirst; you touched me, and I burned to know your peace.[4]

Of all the devotional works written during the medieval period, none has achieved the lasting popularity of Thomas à Kempis' *Imitation of Christ*. Here is Thomas' description of the quest:

> Whoever loves God knows well the sound of his voice. A loud cry in the ears of God is that burning love of the soul which exclaims, "My God and my love, you are all mine and I am yours." Deepen your love in me, O Lord. Let your love possess and raise me above myself with a fervor and wonder beyond imagination. Let me sing the song of love. Let my soul spend itself in your praise, rejoicing for love.[5]

Teresa of Avila, founder of the Carmelite movement, used a different metaphor.

> The beginner must think of himself as of one setting out to make a garden in which the Lord is to take his delight, yet in soil most unfruitful and full of weeds. His Majesty uproots the weeds and will set good plants in their stead. Let us suppose that this is already done. Like good gardeners, with God's help, we have now to make these plants grow.
>
> Let us consider how this garden can be watered. It can be done in four ways: by taking the water from a well, which costs us much labor; or by a waterwheel and buckets, when the water is drawn by a windlass; or by a stream or brook, which waters the ground much better, so that the gardener's labor is less; or by heavy rain, when the Lord waters it with no labor of ours, a way incomparably better than any of those which have been described.[6]

It would seem appropriate, in such an array of seekers, to add some voices closer to our own day. Amy Carmichael, like Teresa before her, accents the divine initiative.

> There is no need to plead that the love of God shall fill our heart as though he were unwilling to fill us. He is willing as light is willing to flood a room that is opened to its brightness; willing as water is willing to flow into an emptied channel. Love is pressing around us on all sides like air. Cease to resist, and instantly loves takes possession.[7]

C. S. Lewis also downgrades the significance of our human feelings and aspirations.

On the whole, God's love for us is a much safer subject to think about than our love for him. Nobody can always have devout feelings; and even if we could, feelings are not what God principally cares about. Christian love, either toward God or toward man, is an affair of the will. But the great thing to remember is that, though our feelings come and go, his love for us does not.[8]

Let me close this time of listening by paraphrasing the wise words of a preacher whom I heard in St. Giles Cathedral when I was studying in Edinburgh, Scotland, many years ago. He used the imagery not of thirst but of hunger. Spiritual hunger, he said, works just opposite from physical hunger. When we are physically hungry, we eat and satisfy our appetites and cease to be hungry. But when we are spiritually undernourished and are then given a feast of good spiritual food, it makes us hungrier than ever. Thus the more we learn about God's love, the more we want to know; we can't get enough.

The reverse, he said, is also true. When we are physically hungry and miss a meal, our appetite becomes ravenous. But if time passes and we receive no spiritual food, we may lose our appetite for it. So the less we hear of God's word, the less we may feel the need for it. Malnutrition sets in and we cease to care.

It follows that the quest for God, once begun, will pick up strength and intensify as it moves along. At the end of this book I cannot promise that you will find the Holy Grail or even that you will enjoy a spiritual feast. But I can promise you a healthy appetite.

WE WANT GOD HIMSELF

It should now be evident that we are not thirsting for any of the attributes of God—for his self-existence, his self-sufficiency, his infinitude, his immutability, his omniscience and omnipotence, his majesty, or his divine transcendence. We want God himself. Our sources have taught us that we can love him with a burning love, even though he remains invisible. In fact, he gives us our love. He rains it into our hearts. Our love may fluctuate (we are only human), but the Holy Spirit is our Guarantor that it will never fade and disappear.

We have also learned that the God who creates the thirst quenches it. According to Scripture, this quenching, assuaging, or slaking is the work of the Spirit. We furnish the parched throat; He supplies the Living Water.

Now, do we want this quenching love? Do we desire it enough to get on our knees and ask for it? Are we ready to plant the garden Teresa talks about? Then let us forget self and fix our minds on God. "In so much of our prayer," says Reuben A. Torrey, "there is really but little thought of God. Our mind is wandering here and there throughout the world. There is no power in that sort of prayer. But when we really come into God's presence, really meet him face to face in the place of prayer, really seek the things that we desire *from him*, then there is power."[9]

I suggest that you read aloud the following lines from Frederic W. H. Myers' poem, "St. Paul":

> Then with a ripple and a radiance through me
> Rise and be manifest, O Morning Star!
> Flow on my soul, thou Spirit, and renew me,
> Fill with thyself, and let the rest be far.

And then these lines which describe the moment when the apostle thirsts no more:

> Oh could I tell ye surely would believe it!
> Oh could I only say what I have seen!
> How should I tell or how can ye receive it,
> How, till he bringeth you where I have been?[10]

Compare those words with the confession of a minister whom I heard during a revival in Canada in 1971: "I don't care what God thinks of my preaching. I'm interested only in those people I see out in front of me. They're the ones I'm trying to impress." That same night he asked to be prayed for. Friends gathered around him, knelt, laid their hands on him, and interceded for him before the throne of God. He in turn quietly asked to be crucified with his Lord and to be filled with the Holy Spirit. And the same God who laid bare the parched and dusty plains of the pastor's heart sent the rain from heaven by the hand of his beloved Son.

The man who received help that night was not a hypocrite; to the contrary, he was an honest person. He simply yearned to get past the church suppers and budget committee meetings to the God of the burning bush; and when he found it impossible, he quit trying. I suspect that more than one lover of God in ancient Israel had the same problem. More than one may have wanted to see the Glory of the Lord in the temple, but was fogged out by the smoke of incense and overwhelmed by the stench of burning animals.

For several years some of us have seen a prayer ministry (known as the "Afterglow") used to create a spiritual hunger and thirst in Christians. People seated in a circle are given an opportunity to ask for prayer, and then are prayed for, with laying-on of hands. Many times a pastor has been surprised when the people who asked for prayer as the Canadian minister did proved to be some of his finest people. These were the church leaders who are always giving of themselves, taking responsibility, providing help above and beyond the call of duty.

Why did they feel the need for prayer? Because while they were praying for others, they caught a glimpse of the Unutterable Beauty. They reached out and touched the hem of the Master's garment. They craved more. They wanted to ascend to a different plane, beyond the edge of self, into God's own territory. They wanted an approach to the Unapproachable, access to the Inaccessible.

"When I speak of God," says Arthur James Balfour, "I mean a God whom men can love, a God to whom men can pray."[11] The mindless religious patter that fills out our church life—not to speak of our religious television programming—can now be seen in its proper perspective.

Lewis is right in saying that it is safer to talk about God's love for us than ours for him. Yet the message of God's everlasting love has been preached since the days of Jeremiah with little enough effect on the course of men and nations. Love that is not returned, unrequited love, is a dead-end street, as many of us have learned in the theater of human experience.

What we need, to paraphrase Franz Delitzsch, the Bible

scholar, is a soul that loves God after the manner of the Psalmist. If the Lord's Presence is vague and unreal, we must raise a thirst. Once we do, we can turn to the pages of the New Testament and read again the words of Jesus: "Blessed are those who hunger and thirst for righteousness, for they will be filled."[12]

But how do we raise a thirst?

CHAPTER THREE

Where Is He?

My tears have been my
food day and night,
while men say to me all day long,
"Where is your God?"
—Psalm 42:3

THE WRONG QUESTION

During the eighteenth century, fur traders from Siberia known as *promyshleniki* raided the Aleutian islands in their quest for sea otter. Frequently they invaded the Aleut villages, slaughtered the men, and seized and raped the women.

If questioned about their behavior they would say, "God is in heaven and the Czar is far away." It didn't occur to them to deny God's existence; they simply located him with the Czar—far away.

Some such theological posture seems to be reflected in this verse. The mockers who kept asking the Psalmist "Where is your God?" were not really atheists, in the opinion of many who have studied the intellectual climate of the ancient world. Rather, the man who, according to Psalms 14 and 53, said in his heart, "There is no God," actually intended to convey, "No God is here."

Serious doubts about the existence of God apparently did not arise in force until the time of the Greek philosophers. No arguments on the question "Is there a God?" will be found either in the Old Testament or in the New.

In his book *Our Knowledge of God,* John Baillie of Edinburgh wrote, "According to the teaching of our Lord, what is wrong with the world is precisely that it does not believe in God. Yet it is clear that the unbelief which he so bitterly deplored was not an intellectual persuasion of God's nonexistence. Those whom he rebuked for their lack of faith were not men who denied God with the top of their minds, but men who, while apparently incapable of doubting him with the top of their minds, *lived* as though he did not exist."[1]

Professor Baillie makes a persuasive case for the claim that people who insist that they don't believe in God really do, as he says, in "the bottom of their hearts." Ninety-six percent of North Americans, it is said, profess to believe in God. So when in company with the Psalmist we are confronted by scoffers who ask, "Where is your God?" we don't need to dredge up the old ontological, cosmological, or teleological arguments for his existence, or to engage in the tiresome debates that surrounded them. Apparently God's *existence* is not the issue. His *whereabouts* is what really concerns people.

But according to Scripture, to ask "Where?" is still the wrong question. It can only lead to foolish speculation. To ask "Why?" on the other hand is legitimate, correct, and scriptural. In our two Psalms the question "Why?" occurs ten times. Job, Moses, David, Jeremiah, and even our Lord asked "Why?" But not once "Where?"

"Where was your God when my son was shot and killed in France?" a distraught father demanded of his pastor during the First World War, and he was told, "He was in the same place that he was when his own Son was killed at Calvary."

And where was that "place?" The Christian dare not pursue that question, for it is a human right he has voluntarily yielded forever. "How unsearchable are his judgments, and his paths beyond tracing out!"[2] But like the Psalmist, we can ask "Why?" and then weep. For us to rummage about in the things of God that are too high for us is not safe. As Martin Luther said, "We must abstain from the curious searching of God's Majesty, which is intolerable to man's body and much more to his mind."[3]

To spill out our usual human impulsiveness here, to assert confidently that we can solve the problem that was too much for the Psalmist, is to strain our intellectual moorings. The verification principle and the laws of non-contradiction and cause-and-effect will not help us. We just don't know why things happen the way they do, or why God permits them, and we might as well candidly admit it.

"It's not easy to be a believer," C. S. Lewis told me during an interview in 1963. "Every war, every shipwreck, every cancer case, every calamity, contributes to making a *prima facie* case against Christianity."[4] To which might be added earthquakes, epidemics, pestilence, insect plague, famine, fire, flood, drought, revolution, armed invasion, tyranny, technological accidents, falling meteors, highway carnage, murder, torture, immorality, pollution, inflation, kidnaping, blackmail . . .

But—we have faith. God is to us as he was to the great ones of the Old Testament, a God of love, justice, and mercy. He is kind and long-suffering, and his deepest desire is that we should not die, but live.

"Do I take any pleasure in the death of the wicked? declares the Sovereign Lord. Rather, am I not pleased when they turn from their ways and live?"[5]

Seek good, not evil, that you may live. Then the Lord God Almighty will be with you.[6]

"Come, all you who are thirsty,
come to the waters;
and you who have no money,
come, buy and eat!
Come, buy wine and milk
without money and without cost.
Why spend money on what is not bread,
and your labor on what does not satisfy?
Listen, listen to me, and eat what is good,
and your soul will delight in the richest of fare.
Give ear and come to me;
hear me, that your soul may live."[7]

This is the medicine we need. Had I been in exile with the Psalmist, sitting with him perhaps at the foot of Mount Hermon, I might, at one time, have tried to blow down the opposition with rational argument and theological expression. No longer. Now I might lay a hand on my friend's shoulder and weep with him and ask God, "Why?"

WHY TEARS?

People in the late twentieth century—ordinary people—do a lot of crying. Sometimes our tears are tears of joy, as when loved ones are reunited to us. As "Silent Night" was being sung at a Christmas Eve service recently, I found myself weeping in church. But more often our tears are tears of pain and grief and despair. Ours is a cruel age, and while we may be considered fortunate, still, for millions of us the pursuit of happiness is over. We have lost the race.

There is much crying in the Psalms. In the Eightieth Psalm, attributed to Asaph, God is reproached on behalf of the people:

You have fed them with the bread of tears;
you have made them drink tears by the bowlful.[8]

Weeping can be nothing more than an exercise in self-pity, for the temptation to bemoan our lot is all too real. But when the Psalmist weeps, it is not just for himself. He identifies with his people, with the human condition, which is why we love him.

Perhaps it is time to look around and assess our own situation. We note first off that whatever the immediate international or domestic crisis, our freedoms are still intact, the democratic system still works, and our standard of living remains the highest in the world. If half of North America's wealth were stripped away, she would still be the envy of the other five continents.

What, then, is wrong? Why tears? Why is the evening newscast one long jeremiad of woe? As a journalist I am familiar with the basis for selecting news stories and therefore refuse to be upset by everything I read and hear. As a Christian I know, too, that no society will ever rid itself completely of crime, graft, or corruption: they came with the package of original sin. The acrimony and bickering that fill our public halls unfortunately are part of the democratic process.

But after every concession has been made to human weakness and the ebb and flow of history and all the other contingencies, we have to admit that something is wrong in the contemporary picture. A malaise has gripped our people during the last twenty years, and it seems to be getting worse. This acute discontent is not rooted in shortages; it was there before the shortages appeared. It is not based on poverty; on the contrary, added income seems to aggravate the condition, which in turn spurs the demand for still more money. It is directed at no one "system," has no single cause, and yet it's there.

Symptoms of the malaise are all around: alcoholism, drug addiction, divorce, pornography, child abuse, homosexuality, witchcraft, promiscuity, rape, incest, violence in the streets and the schools, overcrowded prisons, and the increasing use of indecent language that was taboo in public even five years ago. Thirteen hundred new cults and thousands of messiahs have arisen since 1965. Despite the legislation of recent years, racial discrimination and unrest are still with us, while a feeling of anger and helplessness pervades the electorate as it sees our natural resources petering out with no one able to do a thing about it. And all these symptoms simply point to something deeper.

Two things need to be said about our malaise. First, there is no necessity for it. God never intended it. Psalm 33:12 reads, "Blessed is the nation whose God is the LORD." The cure for national unhappiness is a renewed faith in God. No individual and no people can at the same time be filled with God and filled with gloom. No battery can run down while it is being charged; nor can the eyes look down while they are looking up.

Second, the Christian church exists to minister to the malaise. We can thank God for the vitality of the evangelical churches, for the evangelical upturn is one of the significant developments of recent years. Yet the irony of our situation is that we are not helping to cure the malaise. I say it sadly, but we evangelicals have often become part of the sickness. Instead of becoming ministering physicians to the national soul, we have become contributors to the social deterioration.[9] I do not point the finger, because God's finger is pointed at me; I am as guilty as any. Nor do I pretend to carry an answer in my pocket; I have no blueprint to save a nation.

But when I hear it said in Washington that America's three major industries are Exxon, General Motors, and the illegal importation of marijuana, I am ready to sit with the Psalmist and drink tears by the bowlful. My prayer is "God have mercy on us," for obviously we have nowhere else to turn.

H. Shelton Smith once declared in a lecture that Western culture could be saved only by a "hard-bitten, psalm-singing band of religious revivalists." Where are they? I don't see them at the airports or in the churches. America's founding fathers granted tax exemption to the churches to separate church and state, but they also had another purpose in mind. They wanted to encourage the churches to raise the spiritual level of our culture; to be as it were the nation's chaplains. What we are seeing in our day is the exact opposite: the culture is dragging down the churches.

Take one illustration: more and more evangelical ministers' homes are breaking up, and ministers are remarrying without causing even a ripple in their congregations. To single out the ministers or their wives or the congregations for criticism is pointless; we all know that social conditions and pressures are not what they were. We should be helping these brothers and sisters, not condemning them. But I am weeping.

> Oh, that my head were a spring of water
> and my eyes a fountain of tears![10]

The prophet lamented the state of God's people in his day. I lament because in the midst of the boom in evangelical popularity, we Bible people seem to be having so little moral impact, whether on government, education, culture, or entertainment. "I have found a total inability to follow Christ one hundred per cent of the time and serve in the United States Senate," former Senator Harold Hughes of Iowa told me during an interview in Washington just after he announced his resignation. "I have abandoned the public schools," writes a Christian mother, "and am an active volunteer and substitute teacher at our Christian elementary school."

I weep because so few of us Christians see anything to weep about, so busy are we doing our own thing. We talk a great deal about God, but we seem to want to spend so little time with him. Professor Baillie is right: we believe in God with the top of our heads, but we live as though he did not exist.

On the other hand, religion—to use A. W. Tozer's expression—has become "jolly good fun." The feeling among us seems to be that life is so full of hassles, and tragedy is so obviously waiting in the wings, that to keep harping on the negative is to invite a visit from the man in the white coat. And I identify with that feeling. Why major in the drearies? So we look for entertainment—preferably some religious entertainment—that will not offend our Christian sensibilities. We flip the dial around for music and laughter and praising-the-Lord. We're glad to hear about amazing miracles that cause people to clap and jump up and down. We want to be happy in Jesus.

But perhaps I should not be taking this "power dive" into the negative. My name is not Jeremiah. I'm not the weepy sort. "Tears of sorrow, day and night" do not make up my normal routine. Yet, Jesus identified with those who weep and mourn, and if we are to follow him we cannot escape the descent into this valley.

THE FURNACE OF AFFLICTION

There is healing in tears. "Blessed are those who mourn, for they will be comforted."[11] Augustine, in bitter dejection of spirit one day after his long, losing struggle with the claims of Christ, threw himself down under a fig tree in a garden, and as he said, "let the tears gush freely." He added perspicaciously, "These were the streams that proved a sacrifice acceptable to you, my Lord."[12]

It's true. Tears are acceptable in heaven where there are no tears. Tears are life-affirming. Tears are a sign of awakening in the church (you can't yawn and cry simultaneously). Tears are a sign of love, and John points out by implication that no matter how many prayer requests a person makes or how many sacred books he reads, unless he loves, he will never know God.

Tears tell us the way things really are. We live in a vale of tears, and to pretend we don't is to invite disaster. There is a blessed release in tears; there is a sorrow that leads to hope and peace and joy; there is a balm in suffering when Jesus is connected with it.

While you are reading the Forty-second and Forty-third Psalms, read also Psalm 116. It was called the "Psalm of Bataan" during World War II, because the American soldiers trapped in the Philippines—many of whom died amid torture and neglect—found that it spoke to their condition:

> I love the Lord, for he heard my voice;
>   he heard my cry for mercy.
> Be at rest once more, O my soul,
>   for the Lord has been good to you.
> For you, O Lord, have delivered my soul from death,
>   my eyes from tears,
>   my feet from stumbling
> that I may walk before the Lord
>   in the land of the living.

Teresá of Ávila knew the redemptive nature of suffering, which is why she could pray, "Give me trials, Lord. Give me persecutions." Titus Coan, whom God used in the great revival of 1838 on the island of Hawaii, prayed, "Lord, lay on me what you will, only sustain me. Cut any cord but the one that binds me to your cause, to your heart."[13]

The Letter to the Hebrews says daringly that Jesus was made "perfect through suffering."[14] Paul described his own sufferings this way: "I fill up in my flesh what is still lacking in regard to Christ's afflictions."[15] I'm not sure what he meant, but he wasn't talking about water-skiing. It is hard for a Christian to sing, "Every day with Jesus is sweeter than the day before," when he has suffered one shock after another. Yet the message of the New Testament is that we grow through adversity; that suffering may indeed make tomorrow a blessing. Paul reminds us that there is a fellowship of suffering that binds heart to heart as nothing else can. Perhaps when you and I are battered and bruised by life, it is only to be conditioned for better things. We will be saying more about that.

An inspiring benediction in the First Letter of Peter, I notice with some curiosity, is seldom if ever used in our worship services. I will leave you to decide why. In King James English it goes like this: "The God of all grace, who hath called us unto his eternal glory by Christ Jesus, *after that ye have suffered a while,* make you perfect, stablish, strengthen, settle you. To him be glory and dominion for ever and ever. Amen."[16]

What kind of suffering was Peter referring to? There are hints in the New Testament. We know Peter was imprisoned; and the First Letter of Clement, written in A.D. 96, says that Peter underwent "not one or two but many times of anguish."[17] Paul wrote to the Corinthians, "I have been in danger from rivers, in danger from bandits, in danger from my own countrymen, in danger from Gentiles, in danger in the city, in danger in the country, in danger at sea, and in danger from false brothers. I have labored and toiled and have often gone without sleep; I have known hunger and thirst; I have been cold and naked."[18] Evidently the faith of Peter and Paul was hammered out in the furnace of affliction.

I am not suggesting we can earn our way to heaven through suffering and tears. God forbid that we should wrestle or bawl our way to glory. We are saved by the grace of God through faith plus nothing: let that stand for time and eternity. But if we are to be crucified with Christ, we can expect to feel the pain. As Dietrich Bonhoeffer said, cheap grace is no grace at all.

But the Psalm does not end with weeping. A day came when God reached down and dried the tears of the Psalmist. Let us read on.

CHAPTER FOUR

How It Was

These things I remember
as I pour out my soul:
how I used to go with the multitude,
    leading the procession to the house
        of God,
with shouts of joy and thanksgiving
    among the festive throng.
                    —Psalm 42:4

THE HOLY PARADE

It began hilariously in a hailstorm, the happiest, most exciting Christian parade I have ever witnessed. The scene was Bogotá, Colombia, and some seven hundred delegates from twenty-four South American, Central American, and Caribbean countries had come together for a congress on evangelism.

There were Panamanians in hoopskirts, Paraguayans in *ahopoi* jackets with rows of lace and spangles; bearded Mexicans in wide, colorful trousers; Bolivians with *chukas*—woolen caps with ear flaps. On Sunday afternoon they formed a mammoth parade through the streets of the ancient capital. What banner waving! What shouting of Bible verses! What singing of choruses: "*Solamente en Cristo, solamente en El!*" ("Only in Christ, only in Him.") And heading the procession were gleaming squad cars and motorcycle escorts provided by the Bogotá police department, with lights flashing and sirens wailing.

As the parade wound to its climax, nine thousand people gathered in Plaza Simón Bolívar, in the shadow of the venerable *Catedral de Bogotá,* to hear the gospel of Jesus Christ proclaimed from the capitol steps. Two hundred listeners stepped forward at the close to receive Jesus Christ as Savior in public commitment. Hallelujah!

Was it possible that this noble scene, this *gran desfile,* could take place in the year of grace 1969 in Colombia? Incredible! Colombia, the "New Granada" of the *conquistadores,* once the choicest colony of old Spain? Colombia, where the Inquisition burned martyrs to ashes for their faith at Cartagena? Colombia, where only a dozen years before the parade, three hundred evangelicals died at the hands of religious fanatics—some of them buried alive—while scores of evangelical chapels were destroyed?

Yes, it was possible, for here they were in the civic center, shouting John three-sixteen, while their speakers declared boldly, "We're here in the name of Jesus and we're afraid of nothing. *Nada!*" The Psalmist said he led a procession of the multitude like that, going to the house of God with shouts of joy and thanksgiving among the festive throng.

I have seen crowds—not so exuberant, but nevertheless filled with joy and thanksgiving—winding their way to the great stadiums in Johannesburg, Hong Kong, Seattle, Rio de Janeiro, Winnipeg, Detroit, London, New York, and Dallas to hear Evangelist Billy Graham. I have heard half a million Koreans pray together, each in his own way, on an island outside of Seoul. Such memories make my heart glow.

Nothing can compare with the tingling exultation of a truly Spirit-filled service of worship. To come freely into God's house, to sit with other believers, to lift up the songs of Zion, to bow in corporate prayer, to offer tithes, to listen to testimonies to the Spirit's moving power, to hear the unsearchable riches of Christ proclaimed, to partake of the Lord's body, and to see fruit gathered—surely no other experience in life can match such a sacred hour. And when young people season the occasion with their zeal and enthusiasm, a dimension is added that gladdens every heart present.

Different Psalms convey beautiful impressions of the kind of positive, exhilarating worship atmosphere the Psalmist says he remembers.

> How lovely is your dwelling place,
>   O Lord Almighty!
> My soul yearns, even faints
>   for the courts of the Lord;
> my heart and my flesh cry out
>   for the living God.[1]

What a thrill it was for him to find friends who felt about worship as he did.

> I rejoiced with those who said to me,
>   "Let us go to the house of the Lord."

We are given a unique description of the colorful parade to the temple.

> Your procession has come into view, O God,
>   the procession of my God and King into the sanctuary.
> In front are the singers, after them the musicians;
>   with them are the maidens playing tambourines.
> Praise God in the great congregation;
>   praise the Lord in the assembly of Israel.
> There is the little tribe of Benjamin, leading them,
>   there the great throng of Judah's princes,
>   and there the princes of Zebulon and of Naphtali.
> You are awesome, O God, in your sanctuary.[3]

And then during the service, after they went inside:

> Within your temple, O God,
>   we meditate on your unfailing love.
> Like your name, O God,
>   your praise reaches to the ends of the earth.[4]

"These things I remember," says Psalm 42:4, "as I pour out my soul." Again and again in the Psalms the memory of God's gracious provision in the past is rekindled, causing the spirit to soar. Let us try it.

CALLING THE ROLL

Let's begin by calling up some of the choice names of church history—roll the projector of our minds, as it were, with some quick cuts of the great heroes of our faith. I will list these people, but don't try to read all their names; many of them you may not recognize. Just let them flash past your eyes in rapid succession as a collage, and perhaps they will kindle an impression (which is all we want) of the kingdom and the power and the glory.

We see Moses standing before Pharaoh Rameses II, Elijah before King Ahab, John the Baptist before Herod Antipas and his wife, Herodias; our Lord standing before Pontius Pilate, Peter and John before the Sanhedrin, Paul before King Herod Agrippa and Berenice, Joan of Arc before the Bishop of Beauvais, John Hus before the Bishop of Constance, Luther before Emperor Charles V, Latimer and Ridley before Mary Tudor, Niemoeller before Hitler, Archbishop Luwum before Idi Amin.

Now let's think of the men and women whose writings of devotion have so enriched the life of the church. We begin with the Psalmist himself, then the author of the Odes of Solomon, followed by Clement of Alexandria, Augustine, Bernard of Clairvaux, Lady Julian, Dante, Tauler, Thomas à Kempis, Luis de Leon, Fénélon, Francis de Sales, Milton, Bunyan, John of the Cross, Pascal, Law, Brainerd, Madame Guyon, Amy Carmichael, Samuel Chadwick, Andrew Murray, Watchman Nee, Thomas Kelly—and so many more!

Then let us call up for remembrance the great voices of evangelism, the soul-winners of the past: John Chrysostom,

Savonarola, Fox, Whitefield, Wesley, Finney, Henry Alleine, Moody, William Booth, his daughter (the Maréchale), Wilbur Chapman, John Sung, Sundar Singh, Geoffrey Fletcher, and so many others.

And let us look fleetingly at the great revivals in the history of the church: in Scotland (Kirk o' Shotts, Cambuslang, the Hebrides), in England (Kingswood, Moorfields), in Wales, Nova Scotia, Hawaii, Madagascar, China, Korea, Norway, the Society Islands, the Solomon Islands, East Africa, America (the Great Awakening of 1740; Fulton Street, New York; Los Angeles, 1949) and western Canada, and other places.

Now let us call the roll of some of the missionaries who took part in the most magnificent Christian enterprise of all: the carrying of the Gospel of Jesus Christ to the ends of the earth. First the disciples of Jesus themselves, then the apostles, then such pioneers as Columba, Kentigern, Patrick, Ninian, Ansgar, Ulfilas, Xavier, Veniaminov, Eliot, Nommensen, Las Casas, Carey, Judson, Morrison, Gilmour, Williams, Mackay, J. G. Paton, Mary Slessor, Marcus and Narcissa Whitman, Livingstone, Coillard, Sheldon Jackson, Underwood, Goforth, and Kenneth Strachan.

Well, that's enough; we can stop the projector. Important as these people and places have been to the life of the church, few of them matter to us today. Did the list seem long? Actually it was pathetically short and incomplete. Before these people, with them, and after them came many whose names I neglected to mention, together with myriads of unsung faithful ones whose names we will never know in this life. They loved Jesus and sought to serve him. As we pour out our souls, let us remember them and thank God that their names are written in heaven.

WHAT ABOUT NOW?

Our Psalmist says, "I *used to* go to the house of God." In his apparent exile, he is in a state of recollecting, and that's where we are in this book. We have been thinking of the church's triumphs in the past. What can we say about the present?

By missionaries, by crusades, by seminars, by translation

teams, by fraternal workers, by relief agencies, by pastors' conferences, by specialists, by television, by radio, by satellite, by cassettes, by recordings, by films, by computers, by tracts, by books and magazines, by telephone, by ships, by newspaper advertising, by billboards, by smuggling, by balloons, by floating bottles, by every means conceivable—and some inconceivable—the Gospel is going out in our time.

Some doors are closing. New restrictions on Christians are being put into effect in Afghanistan, Angola, Cambodia, Ethiopia, Iran, Israel, Laos, Mozambique, Vietnam, and parts of India. Still other doors remain closed. The word *missionary* is considered a synonym for *imperialism* by the politicians of the Third World. One could easily predict that in many areas, by the year 2000, the holy procession to the house of God—to use the Psalmist's figure—will be broken up by Arab oil or Russian-built tanks. Should the Lord delay his return, the work of spreading the Gospel will be harder, resistance will be fiercer, and Christians will be martyred and massacred by the thousands.

But it would be completely false to say that therefore the spreading of the Gospel of Jesus Christ will cease. God's purposes are not easily thwarted. Long ago Tertullian wrote that blood is seed. Government efforts to halt the work of evangelism have never succeeded totally since Peter and the apostles stood before the Sanhedrin (as reported in Acts 5) and said, "We must obey God rather than men."

In recent years certain sending agencies have reported more missionary opportunities than ever, and more workers are being trained and moving out. Uganda, a scene of bitter persecution for eight years, is now open to Christian workers. The People's Republic of China, closed since midcentury, is being penetrated by Chinese evangelists from Hong Kong; it is a hidden work but it is expanding. And an Indian Christian, with offices both in India and America, has managed to post Russian Bibles from India to subscribers to the Moscow telephone directory.

The ingenuity, the zeal, the aggressiveness of today's young Christians is astonishing. A new breakthrough in the mass media means to them a fresh channel for communicating the Gospel of Jesus. You can't stop them and you can't keep them out! The missionary enterprise of the Victorian era was magnificent, but the evangelistic effort of the church in our time is broader in scope and even more remarkable. To present Christ to every human being is now considered by some to be a practical, attainable goal.

And yet . . .

Assets must be weighed against liabilities. The problem of the church goes deeper than the drops in membership in many denominations, the withdrawal of some missionary forces, the decline of Sunday School enrollment, the lag in baptisms and new church developments, and other measurable criteria.

On the surface our churches look healthy enough. We still have freedom to preach; Bibles are open; our church lawns are well kept (evangelicals are not as poor as they used to be). We take more trips to the mission field and the Holy Land; we jet back and forth to conferences on church renewal; we hire specialized counselors and church growth experts to improve our image in the community.

Underneath, however, our churches are being molded little by little by the subtle changes taking place in society— changes that are hard to describe but very real. The malaise of America has spread like a smog into many churches and has affected the morale of some of their young people.

Outside the churches, too many young people are losing their sense of traditional values and are substituting another kind of philosophy. They have become convinced that the present social structure is rotten to the core and not worth defending; that crime does in fact pay; that going on welfare is better than working; and that success is not the way to the good life.

To go to South America, rent an airplane, and fly a load of illegal drugs to Arizona has become an appealing prospect. It means friends, flashy cars, Las Vegas. And so at the cinema, the racetrack, the drag strip, the bar, the theater, the concert, and even the university, this philosophy is being peddled and many are being corrupted.

Parents stand around bewildered, aware that something is terribly wrong but unable to put their finger on it. The evangelical leadership is fully cognizant that Satan is busy destroying our youth wherever he can, but usually we are isolated from the sin centers. Besides, to be frank, many of our churches are taken up at the moment straightening out problems in the choir and blacktopping our parking lot. "Bringing in the sheaves" could be termed a long-range goal.

What is missing? God? But that can't be. We talk about God all the time.

Ah yes, but do we thirst after him? Do we say with the Psalmist, "My heart and my flesh cry out for the living God"? Jesus said he had overcome the world and its tribulation. Let's see if he can overcome our problems.

CHAPTER FIVE
Remembering

Why are you downcast, O my soul?
  Why so disturbed within me?
Put your hope in God,
  for I will yet praise him
  for the salvation of his face.

—Psalm 42:5

O my God, my soul is downcast within me;
  therefore I will remember you
from the land of the Jordan,
  the heights of Hermon—from Mount Mizar.
—Psalm 42:6

To avoid repetition, verse 42:5 will be discussed in chapter 16 together with its parallel verses, 42:11 and 43:5.

DOWN IN THE PIT

According to topographers, the Jordan valley is the lowest depression on earth. Lake Gennesaret (the Sea of Galilee) is sunk nearly 700 feet below the Mediterranean Sea, and the Dead Sea nearly 1,300 feet. To the north, at the head of the Jordan valley, stands Mount Hermon, highest point in the Holy Land, with a summit rising 9,232 feet (1,954 meters) above sea level. From a point on the lake to the crest of Hermon, one is looking at an elevation of 10,000 feet.

Many commentators have noted a mood change in our Psalm beginning with verses 5 and 6. The poet no longer diets solely on tears, but oscillates like a heart machine with low and high vibrations. For several verses he alternates rhythmically between the valley and the mountain. Then as we move into Psalm 43, he chooses to stay on the mountain. The skilled development of thought and feeling denotes a work of high artistic quality.

Apart from the puzzling reference to Mount Mizar,[1] verse 6 contains four elements: a downcast soul, a depressed region, an elevated peak, and God. We can make an equation of it: a depressed land is to a mountaintop as a depressed soul is to God. If the author was using the geography of the region to point up a contrast, then the challenge of his Psalm to you and me is obvious: we are to get out of the depressed valley and up to the sunlit peaks. Out of the ground fog and river mist and up on the slopes where it's the most natural thing in the world to communicate with God.

But how do we do it? People tell us, "There's only one way to stop being downcast, and that is to look up." We try, but find it's not that easy. So now we're looking at this Psalm, asking what it has to tell us. After all, it is part of God's Word, and we ought to be able to expect help from it.

Well, what does the Psalmist say? He is certainly not waving his shirt from a mountain crag. He is downcast and is remembering God. He is remembering but he is still downcast. He seems far from the heights of Hermon, in a depressed and negative situation that is not exactly bubbling with possibilities.

But wait! Look again. This man is not wearing a religious front. He has dropped his smiling image. Pop religion is not on sale here, nor is easy piety. Someone is honest, open, candid, and leveling with us. He loves God but is not stroking that relationship. Deep in his soul he is hurting.

What a relief! We learn that things are with him the way they are with us, and always have been with a majority of the human race. Let's not hurry away from here. Let's not slip over to another group where the people are swaying to "I've got the joy, joy, joy, joy." Let's stay with the Psalmist: "My soul is downcast within me." This is Scripture. Perhaps later we shall learn some things about spiritual quickening and new life; right now we'll just sit quietly at this sad singer's feet.

He is depressed; so are millions of us. He wants (so it seems) to get up to the heights of Hermon; so do we. Whether his state of depression has a psychological, biochemical, political, or other explanation, we don't know and it doesn't matter. We can't analyze him for guilt feelings or repressed hostility, and if we could it wouldn't help. The true value of the Forty-second Psalm is not its autobiographical content (which is slim enough) but the mirror it holds up to our own souls.

Let's test the Scriptures to see whether this man is unique, or whether other downcast spirits may be found in God's Word.

Consider Moses, an exile and fugitive from justice, wandering in the desert, old and forgotten.[2]

Joshua, morose and dejected because his crossing of the Jordan resulted in military defeat.[3]

Hannah, downhearted, unable to eat, a victim of cheap remarks because she was unable to bear children.[4]

Elijah, fearful of his life, fleeing into the desert, alone and miserable.[5]

Naaman, the Syrian general, crushed to find himself a leper.[6]

The widow of Nain, distracted by grief over the loss of her only son.[7]

The wild man of Gadara, so despondent over his plight that he was mutilating himself.[8]

The woman by the lake shore, worn out by incompetent doctors and twelve years of hemorrhaging.[9]

Bartimaeus, blind, sitting wretched and disconsolate near the Jericho gate, begging.[10]

The unhappy man at the pool of Bethesda, invalided for thirty-eight years with no one to help him.[11]

Jesus at Calvary.

Peter, lying in prison, bound in chains and guarded by four Roman soldiers.[12]

The crew of the frail barque on which Paul was traveling as a prisoner, in despair of their lives during heavy seas off Malta.[13]

Others could be cited from the Scripture, each of whom, struggling against weighty odds, could identify with the Psalmist in his depression of spirit. In the church's arduous pilgrimage through the centuries, how many more could be added!

Including us.

REMEMBERING GOD

But why do we have to talk about being downcast? Who wants the glummies? Isn't there enough trouble in the world without our having to wallow in it? Let's wash our hair, or swallow a pill, or go jogging, or have friends in. Anything to get up the mountain!

Besides, maybe things aren't all that bad. Billy Graham has been preaching behind the Iron Curtain. After being closed for years, church doors are opening in China. Church growth studies of certain denominations show an upward trend. Evangelical seminaries report increasing enrollments. What about those great evangelistic congresses of recent years— don't they tell us something about the power of God at work? And it's reported that 98 percent of all homes in North America have at least one Bible. And that's not all.

Look at this United Press International story out of New York City. It describes a 1978 survey of 21,000 high school juniors and seniors. It states that 81 percent were linked to an organized religion, 76 percent had not had sexual intercourse,

60 percent intended to be virginal when they marry, and 54 percent said they would not live with someone prior to marriage. And—98 percent reported that they had never smoked marijuana.[14]

Of course, these were outstanding young people, chosen for "Who's Who Among Students in American High Schools" on the basis of leadership, scholarship, and community endeavors. But other positive pointer readings can be found in today's Western social order. People are healthier, taller, stronger, and live longer. Infant mortality is down. Diets are better. Lots of good things are happening; why don't we cheer up and stop all this nonsense?

Yes, why don't we? Until recent times cynicism was not as common as it is today. During World War II when someone was complaining too much, we would say, "Go see the chaplain."

In the days that lie ahead we may appreciate better the Psalmist's predicament in the Forty-second Psalm and his response to it. Everything was going downhill for him. Living in exile, perhaps behind a "Berlin wall," perhaps even held as a hostage, he faced a situation whose rawness we have difficulty imagining. Those around him were deriding him for continuing to believe in God. Their jeers must have resembled the shouts outside the American embassy in Teheran. His prayers were not producing results. The future looked grim; God was apparently working no miracles in his vicinity. He kept talking to himself—"Why are you downcast, O my soul?"—but always there was the twit, "Where is your God?"

Another Psalm, the Seventy-seventh, reflects similar feelings.

> I cried out to God for help;
>   I cried out to God to hear me.
> When I was in distress, I sought the Lord;
>   at night I stretched out untiring hands
>   and my soul refused to be comforted.
>
> I remembered you, O God, and I groaned;
>   I mused, and my spirit grew faint.

> You kept my eyes from closing;
>   I was too troubled to speak.
> I thought about the former days,
>   the years of long ago;
> I remembered my songs in the night.
>   My heart mused and my spirit inquired: . . .
> "Will he never show his favor again?
> Has his unfailing love vanished forever? . . .
> Has God forgotten to be merciful?
>   Has he in anger withheld his compassion?"

But now comes his mood change. The time of grieving is over. The music moves into a major key.

> Then I thought, "To this I will appeal:
>   the years of the right hand of the Most High."
> I will remember the deeds of the Lord;
>   yes, I will remember your miracles of long ago.
> I will meditate on all your works
>   and consider all your mighty deeds.

Beware, Satan. This man is about to slip through your outer lines. He was discouraged, but now he is remembering God. He is recalling God's goodness, his mercy, his power. Look for a change; look for a plan of action.

One of my favorite Old Testament stories is found in 1 Samuel 30. David the warrior, with a band of his men, had hired out as a Philistine vassal. While they were in the field they left their families in the city of Ziklag. Upon returning to the city they found that Amalekite troops from the south had invaded the land, had set fire to the city, and departed, apparently taking captive the wives and children. David's men were so furious they were ready to stone their leader.

David was deeply distressed, as well he might have been. It's hard to imagine how things could have been worse for him. The Amalekites were not renowned for their merciful behavior. But instead of putting on sackcloth and making a show of grief, David, we are told, "encouraged himself in the Lord his God."[15] That's all. But within two days he and his men had overtaken the raiders and had rescued all the captive wives and children.

David encouraged himself as the Psalmist did, by remembering what God had done before. He saw that if God did it once, he could do it again; his hand is not shortened that it cannot save. He left this testimony: when we encourage ourselves in the Lord our God, hope begins to bud and faith to blossom.

THE RAVEN BEFORE THE DOVE

In the fall of 1954 I was deeply discouraged, and nothing seemed to help. The church I was pastoring was caught in a neighborhood change. An exciting opportunity for Christian service had opened up and had drifted through my fingers. Unknown forces seemed ranged against me until my health was affected. The future looked dismal and bleak, and I was not getting younger.

An anonymous person had subscribed for me to a magazine that had always irritated me, and when it began arriving it only aggravated my feelings. However, the lead article in one issue attracted my attention on this particular day. It was entitled "Discouragement," and the author was Charles Haddon Spurgeon, a nineteenth-century British preacher whom I greatly admired. I knew that Spurgeon himself was subject to times of depression. The article I read was taken from a lecture he had delivered to the students at his Pastors' College.

"Our work," said Spurgeon, "when earnestly undertaken, lays us open to attacks in the direction of depression. Who can bear the weight of souls without sometimes sinking to the dust? Passionate longings after men's conversion, if not fully satisfied (and when are they?) consume the soul with anxiety and disappointment. To see the hopeful turn aside, the godly grow cold, professors [nominal Christians] abusing their privileges, and sinners waxing more bold in sin—are not these sights enough to crush us to the earth? The Kingdom comes not as we would, the reverend Name is not hallowed as we desire, and for this we must weep. How can we be otherwise than sorrowful, while men believe not our report, and the divine arm is not revealed? . . .

"This depression comes over me whenever the Lord is preparing a larger blessing for my ministry; the cloud is black before it breaks, and overshadows before it yields its deluge of mercy. Depression has now become to me as a prophet in rough clothing, a John the Baptist, heralding the nearer coming of my Lord's richer benison.

"So have better men found it. The scouring of the vessel has fitted it for the Master's use. Immersion in suffering has preceded the baptism of the Holy Ghost. Fasting gives an appetite for the banquet. The Lord is revealed in the backside of the desert, while his servant keeps the sheep and waits in solitary awe. The wilderness is the way to Canaan. Defeat prepares for victory. The raven is sent forth before the dove. The darkest hour of night precedes the dawn."[16]

Spurgeon's words gave me hope simply by getting my mind off myself and on the Lord. I began looking to him. I thought of that great day when the saints will "come marching in" and how we all yearned to be "in that number." I remembered God, and he did not forget me.

Here is a prayer I wrote coming out of that experience, that might be called a prayer of remembrance:

Heavenly Father, I approach you in the Name of your Son. I don't have the right words, it's neither the right time nor the right place; I need to be quiet but there is no quiet.

I will not ask you to deliver me out of my situation because a lot of it was brought on by myself. I will not ask you to fill my cup, for my cup is a sieve. Instead of asking I am remembering.

I remember that you created the universe and all its galaxies by your mighty power, and said it was good. Lord God, let me be part of that good.

I remember that you said I could find you when I sought you with all my heart. Father, at this moment my heart is yours; there is nothing between us.

I remember that you forgave my sins and purchased my salvation with the blood of your Son. I place myself under that blood and claim Jesus Christ as the One who saved me at the Cross.

I remember that you established your church as a fellowship of believers committed to a life of love. Father, put me in your church not as a pew-sitter but as a lover.

I remember that you sent your Spirit into our church to teach us what love is. I need to be taught again.

I remember that your Son is coming back for us one day. Come, Lord Jesus.

I remember that you will keep us in perfect peace if our minds are stayed on you. Father, I love you, adore you, magnify you, praise your Name, and count you more precious than anything in life. And for at least two minutes my mind has been stayed on you.

Because you hear me, I am at peace.

Because you forgive me, I leave my sins.

Because you overcome evil, I drop my fears.

You are my Shield, my Fortress, my Advocate, my Shepherd, my Light, my Wisdom, and my Friend.

I have nothing to ask for, really. Just remembering. Thank you, Father.

Has a black cloud moved in over your life? Get ready! God is about to break it open and shower you with blessings. As John of the Cross, the sixteenth-century Spanish mystic, wrote, there is a divine light that purges and illumines the soul "even when the soul thinks not that it has this light, but believes itself to be in darkness."[17]

Deep is about to call to deep.

CHAPTER SIX

Deep

Deep calls to deep
  in the roar of your waterfalls;
all your waves and breakers
  have swept over me.
          —Psalm 42:7

THE GREAT MYSTERY

When Blaise Pascal died in 1662 A.D. at the age of thirty nine, his valet found sewn into the lining of his coat a crumpled piece of paper. On it the French scientist had jotted some notes of a vision he had experienced eight years before. The time was specified: it was Monday, November 23, 1654, from ten-thirty in the evening until half-past twelve.

Here are the notes as translated:

FIRE

God of Abraham, God of Isaac, God of Jacob, not of the philosophers and savants.

Certitude. Certitude. Feeling, Joy, Peace.

God of Jesus Christ.
My God and your God.
"Your God shall be my God."
Forgetfulness of the world and of everything, except God.
He is to be found only by the ways taught in the Gospel.
Greatness of the soul of man.
"Righteous Father, the world has not known you, but I have known you."
Joy, joy, joy, tears of joy.
I have fallen away from him.
They have forsaken me, the Fountain of living waters.
"My God, will you forsake me?"
May I not fall from him for ever.
"This is life eternal, that they might know you, the only true God, and Jesus Christ, whom you have sent."
Jesus Christ.
Jesus Christ.
I have fallen away: I have fled from him, denied him, crucified him.
May I not fall from him for ever.
We keep hold of him only by the ways taught in the Gospel.
Renunciation, total and sweet.[1]

In the language of the Psalmist, that was "deep calling to deep." The word *deep* in the Old Testament usually refers to deep water, such as the ocean. But the cataracts or waterfalls on Mount Hermon, where some believe this Psalm was written, are nowhere near the ocean or the Mediterranean Sea, nor are they especially high or deep. So the experts are hard put to describe how the Psalmist could slip and fall into a Jordan tributary near its mountain source during the spring runoff, flounder among the boulders, feel the rushing cataracts pouring over his head, imagine he was at the ocean where the waves were breaking, and then write a Psalm about it! My alternative explanation is not so scholarly, but neither it is so acrobatic. It is more like the piece of paper found in Pascal's pocket.

"Deep calling to deep" is the Spirit of God calling to the human spirit. Ray Stedman says there are deeps in God that correspond with the deeps in man.[2] Pascal described them as "motions of grace." What we are considering is the primeval stirring of the Unknown as it moves toward the known. It is the numinous brush of angels' wings, the mysterious "Jesus factor" that aviators sometimes speak of in relating an escape from death. To understand this phenomenon we need to go back to Genesis, to the dawn of creation, when darkness was upon the face of the deep and the Spirit of God moved upon the face of the waters.

A mystery so profound cannot easily be reduced to functionary dimensions—to hand-raising, membership classes, denominational statistics. When deep responds to deep the soul itself is involved. The Unsearchable is searching, by whose knowledge "the deeps were divided."[3] The word of salvation comes to us. Something hidden in the universe is communicating on a wave-length we apprehend but do not understand. Love is winging its way into our hearts and we are overwhelmed.

> You stretched forth your hand from above [wrote Augustine] and drew up my soul from the dark abyss. You lifted me up and I realized there was something to see, but I wasn't quite capable of seeing it. My vision was too weak to stand the radiance of your glory, and I trembled with a combination of love and dread. . . . This was no ordinary light of day, visible to the naked eye; nor was it an intensifying of that light to the nth degree. It was not floating over my mind as oil floats above water, or as the sky is over the earth. Rather it was something altogether different. It was over me because it made me, and I was beneath it because I was made by it. But everyone who knows the truth knows that Light, and he who knows it knows it forever. It is the Light of love.[4]

"Oh, the depths of the riches of the wisdom and knowledge of God!" wrote the apostle Paul. "How unsearchable his judgments, and his paths beyond tracing out."[5]

Deep calls to deep.

BREAKERS AND ROLLERS

But the Psalmist is in desperate plight. "All your waves and breakers have swept over me." The imagery points to a half-drowned struggler in the surf, battered by roller after roller in rapid succession. I can think of more than one evangelical brother and sister, and more than one evangelical church, in exactly that situation—pelted by blow after blow with no end in sight.

You might say the Psalmist's predicament was an occupational hazard. He lived in a primitive society always on the edge of crisis, prey to enemies roundabout, subject to the whims of wind and weather. Trouble was his life.

But what about us? We're not in such straits. We ought to be the happiest people in this best of all possible worlds. We live in the most prosperous nation in history, protected from invasion for 160 years, boasting the strongest military might, with more colleges, more churches, more missionaries than any other country. An astonishing 30 percent of our population attends church. We are the best-fed, best-educated, best-cared-for, most tolerant, most generous people—or so we have been led to believe.

Yet I can show you churches where there has not been a single accession to the membership upon confession of faith or baptism for the past five years—scores of them! Not only that, but the congregation is divided, the leadership is in disarray, the minister's salary is in arrears, and waves are breaking all over the place.

If you were to ask the people in these churches what they want, many of them would tell you, "We don't want a religious club with a revolving door. We don't want explanations of things totally unrelated to our lives. We want God!"

"If we would find God amid all the religious externals," wrote A. W. Tozer, "we must first determine to find him, and then proceed in the way of simplicity. When religion has said its last word, there is little that we need other than God himself."[6] What is the "way of simplicity"? Is it not getting rid of secondary goals, unloading the excess baggage of our minds, and going after the big prize?

We need to seek God for his own sake, not for what he can do for us. Not for blessing, or fulfillment, or sharing, or service to others. As I suggested earlier, let's put aside these for the time being and not ask him for one thing; let's just take that verse, "Be still and know that I am God," and stay with it.

Young Spurgeon was converted when he heard a minister preach on the text, "Look unto me and be ye saved, all the ends of the earth; for I am God, and there is none else." Let's look at God as Jesus Christ made him known to us. Do we not see him? How do we know we do not? We have scarcely begun to look. Jesus said, "Seek, and you will find."[7]

You protest, "I hardly know what I am looking for, and how can I tell when I've found it?" Well, that seems a good opening for a Bible story. In the Garden of Eden stood two trees. The first man and the first woman ate the forbidden fruit of one; they never got to the other. The tree they robbed was the tree of the knowledge of good and evil. The tree they left untouched was the tree of life. As a consequence, their descendants have lived unhappily ever since with the knowledge of good and evil. But somehow the knowledge of Life— the Life that our Creator intended us to have—has eluded us.

Jesus never spoke of the first tree, as far as the record shows, but he said something about the second one that should be read by every believer whether his soul is downcast or not. He said, "He who has an ear, let him hear what the Spirit says to the churches. To him who overcomes, I will give the right to eat from the tree of life, which is in the paradise of God."[8]

In Genesis 3:22, after Adam and Eve had eaten from the tree of the knowledge of good and evil, the Lord God himself banished them from Eden with the words, "The man . . . must not be allowed to reach out his hand and take also from the tree of life and eat, and live forever." But now Jesus is saying that "overcomers" will have the right to the fruit of that same tree which is today standing in Paradise, and from which our first parents were once forbidden to eat.

What a thrill! What an honor! What a privilege! And what a goal for the church: to make itself into a gateway to the tree of life. Instead of just welcoming people at the door and showing them to a pew, we can show them into the orchard—not the garden from which our parents were banished, but one into which Jesus has invited us through his cross: This is the Garden of Eternal Life, Paradise, in the midst of which stands the tree of life, whose leaves are for the healing of the nations.

THERE IS AN ESCAPE

What waves were breaking over the Psalmist, what cataracts were pounding in his ears, we shall not know in this life. Yet we cannot help feeling a certain empathy with him. His metaphors speak to our condition, three thousand years later.

Look again at some of our own waves: the nuclear threat is rising, the arms race is intensifying, radiation and cancer are spreading, pollution is increasing, energy is running out, the ocean is dying, ozone is disappearing, terrorism and crime are spreading, cults are multiplying, democracy is shrinking. Suicide is taking an increasing toll among the young. The secular view has been nutshelled by novelist Kurt Vonnegut in these terrible words: "Things are going to get worse and worse and never get better again."

If it seems that I am suddenly turned pessimist again and am distorting the true situation, I am only reflecting the Psalmist's view of his own generation, as he expressed it in Psalm 14:

> The Lord looks down from heaven
>   on the sons of men
> to see if there are any who understand,
>   any who seek God.
> All have turned aside,
>   they have together become corrupt;
> there is no one who does good,
>   not even one.[9]

In counseling with young people about God's "plan" for their lives, we might add a touch of realism by having them read the Forty-second Psalm. Then we could tell them that more martyrs have died for the cause of Jesus Christ in the twentieth century than in all the previous nineteen centuries together. We could tell them about the believers who were baptized in their own blood in Korea, Kenya, Chad, Uganda, Lithuania, Poland, Ukraine, China, Vietnam, Cambodia, and a score of other countries, just in the past few years.

Is that all there is, then? A life once described by Thomas Hobbes as "solitary, poor, nasty, brutish and short"? Or is there something better?

Years ago I read a German story about a middle-aged housewife of whom it was said, "The greater the clamor and turmoil around her, the calmer she became within." Any climber knows that back of the waterfall is a place of calm and safety. We have to go through the waterfall to get to it, but once there, we have escaped the force of the cataract. That place is where God is.

We cannot escape the world by slipping off to the desert as the monks did; the desert is now an atomic proving ground. We cannot wander into a quiet churchyard as Thomas Gray did to compose his elegy; the churchyard is now a traffic island surrounded by freeways. But we can retire to where God is, inside the waterfall. We can surround ourselves with the thoughts of people who have thought much of God. "Come near to the holy men and women of the past," writes Tozer, "and you will soon feel the heat of their desire after God. They mourned for him, they prayed and wrestled and sought for him day and night, and when they had found him the finding was all the sweeter for the long seeking."[10]

There is a life that is out of the range of airplanes, truck routes, drag strips, and Muzak. It is a life, not of total silence, but of pleasant sounds: the rustle of the wind, the whirr of hummingbirds, the tinkle of laughter, the singing of God's praises. It is life in the Spirit, unhurried, simple, serene, amazing, radiant, triumphant. Is it "involved"? Yes. But the greater the clamor without, the more placid the calm within.

In the pages that lie ahead we shall discover, God willing, that those who are filled with the Spirit lose the bitter, ragged edge of existence. Injustice is still there; spilled blood is still there; but life doesn't overwhelm us any more than it overwhelmed those who died for the name of Jesus. As Thomas Kelly says, "We need not get frantic. He is at the helm."[11]

CHAPTER SEVEN

A Song

_____

By day the Lord directs his love,
at night his song is with me—
a prayer to the God of my life.
—Psalm 42:8

_____

FAITH IS NO RISK

In *A Diary of Evolution in a Small Country Town*, written during World War I, Jane Mander describes her pilgrimage from faith to no faith. I quote two excerpts:

Age 5-12: Accept Bible as written, God, Christ and the angels in toto, Fixed Heaven and Hell, the Good and the Bad.

Age 35-36: A great weariness. Sick of action. Sick of words.
Sick of humanity. No illusions left. Shed everything. Do
nothing.[1]

When the Psalmist says, "At night his song is with me," he is
talking precisely about what Jane Mander says she lost between the ages of twelve and thirty-six: faith. The song is a
prayer, and prayer is the language of faith. In the morning of
her life as a young girl, Jane Mander apparently enjoyed a
childlike trust in the goodness of God. As she entered the
second half of life, the darkness fell, the fog settled in, and it
was night.

For most Christians it is normal to take a hopeful view of
life by day when the sun is shining. All is bright and clear and
coming up roses. We see what we need and what we have to
do. Health, vigor, opportunity seem to be the important issues. God's in his heaven and is directing his love. Things are
in good hands; we can get to work.

But the nighttime is a different story. No longer is God's
love plainly seen. Situations that would not trouble us by day
(a telephone call would take care of it) now appear monstrous.
We become confused and panicky. We arrive home late with
a feverish child to find that the house has been burglarized,
the power is off, the car insurance company has sent a cancel-
lation notice, the checking account is overdrawn, the garbage
collectors are on strike, there's a legal notice—and what else?

Existence appears an intolerable burden. We are overcome
by weariness—or terror. Life has turned rancid. Yet we have
to do something, and the question is, What? It is at this point
in time, at this moment of crisis, the Psalmist says, that God
sends a song.

> I will sing of the mercies of the Lord forever,
> I will sing . . . I will sing.[2]

Faith, according to the Letter to the Hebrews, "is being sure
of what we hope for and certain of what we do not see."[3] It's
hard to see in the dark. What we need is a light. And what
light does faith provide for our predicament? The light of
God's Word. His word is "a lamp to my feet and a light for my

path."[4] George Mueller wrote, "The province of faith begins where probabilities cease and sight and sense fail. Appearances are not to be taken into account. The question is—whether God has spoken it in his Word."[5]

Theodore Greene has defined faith as "whole-hearted belief on the basis of evidence, but not wholly conclusive evidence, and of interpretation which is reasonable but which falls short of absolute proof."[6] In other words, faith is a risk worth taking, an uncertain venture into the Grand Perhaps. With all deference to Professor Greene, that is not biblical faith. "The faith that saves is not a conclusion drawn from evidence; it is a moral thing, a thing of the Spirit, a supernatural infusion of confidence in Jesus Christ, a very gift of God. Faith is a miracle; it is the ability God gives to trust his Son."[7]

Notice how Greene's definition comes short of Mueller's. Faith for Mueller is conditioned not by good odds, but by the fact that "God has spoken." That is biblical faith. Faith is not wishing, hoping, gambling, whistling in the dark, hypothesizing, surmising, pining, or opining. Faith is sure conviction, resting in dependence upon God. It is a scriptural fact. Moreover, it is a song: "I know that my Redeemer lives."

In Psalm Twenty-three are the familiar words,

> Even though I walk
>   through the valley of the shadow of death,
> I will fear no evil,
>   for you are with me.

"You are with me" is not hope; it is absolute certainty. It is biblical faith, based on divine revelation and proven realities.

Does such a faith ignore the blunt truth about our confused situation? No. Does it disregard the pain and agony that Jane Mander went through, leading to her disillusionment about life? In no way. Faith takes a realistic look at the conditions of existence and never assumes that if we believe something hard enough, it will come to pass. Faith actually rests on a Word from beyond itself: "We know that in all things God works for the good of those who love him, who have been called according to his purpose."[8]

Little Jane Mander, as she relates it, had a love song in the morning of her life. Then darkness seemed to fall during her mid-thirties, and the song faded. Only faith will give it back.

LOVE IS THE BADGE

In the fifth chapter of Galatians, King James Version, appear four portentous words: "Faith . . . worketh by love." The New International Version is more contemporary: "The only thing that counts is faith expressing itself through love."[9] The Psalmist tells us that "by day the Lord directs his love." What then is this love?

Love is not something apart from God, for God is love. He is love even if there is no one around to be loved. He is love before he loves us and without his loving us, and he loves us just because he is love.

According to Scripture, love is the badge by which God's people áre to be recognized. A thousand years after the Psalmist, Jesus said, "All men will know that you are my disciples if you love one another."[10] The First Letter of John says that love is the sign that God's children have passed from death to life; from which we conclude that love is the mark of the true church, and where there is no love, there is no church. The congregation becomes just another religious conglomeration.

"By day the Lord directs his love." God is the Creator of everything in nature except sin, and he directs his love toward everything he has made. And while all his creatures are embraced in his love, the Bible tells us that God made human beings in his own image. We are special—not special in ourselves, but special in God. Christoph Blumhardt once said, "Our life has no meaning in itself; it has meaning only in relation to God."[11]

What kind of love is it that God shows toward us? The Old Testament writers declare that God's love is personal, voluntary, spontaneous, undeserved, jealous, sometimes severe, sometimes tender, but always long-suffering and compassionate. As for the other Testament, "All that the New Testament has to say about the love of God to men," says C.E.B. Cranfield, "is expressed in the two words, 'Jesus Christ.'"[12]

To say that God is love raises ago-old questions. Where does hate come from? Does love inflict pain? Is God just, or is he merciful? Can the two be reconciled? To such questions the Psalmist does not give answer. The "mystery of iniquity" remains a mystery. What he does tell is that not only is God love, but he loves *us*. It is *his* song that is with us.

When we ask how a man downcast in soul and battered by the waves of circumstance can come up with the Lord's song, we find an answer in Romans 5:5: "God has poured out his love into our hearts by the Holy Spirit, whom he has given us." Faith works by love, and love is what the Holy Spirit brings us.

If we could drive our thinking out of the dim circular ramps of unbelief and onto the open expressway of God's truth, we might begin to understand that to be filled with the Holy Spirit is to be filled with love. And when we have understood that, we have understood Jesus.

What do we know about the Holy Spirit? He is God, and since God is love, the Holy Spirit is love. He is the One Jesus promised to send, the Paraclete who would lead us into all truth. And the truth is that the universe was made for love and in love.

But what is love? Is it power? No, quintessentially love is neither physical nor social nor psychic nor religious power. In fact, it has nothing to do with power as humanity normally understands and uses it.

Love is not lust. The Greek word *eros* (desire) never appears in the Bible. Love and lust are simply not in the same camp—which the world has never understood. Love appreciates the flesh, enjoys the flesh, but refuses to give it priority. Take an illustration from Scripture: David and Jonathan loved each other with a mature but innocent love.[13] Their kind of love—and it is still common today—leaves sodomy in Sodom.

Love is not self-gratification. Many people use the language of love when their sole aim is to bend others to their selfish desires. A character in one of Graham Greene's novels complains, "You keep saying love-love-love, but all I hear is I-I-I."

Because someone once did, or may some day do something nice for me, I may feel loving toward him. But by New Testament measurement that is not a sufficient basis for love.

Love is not blindness. It is not so intoxicated by its object that it violates the canons of responsible behavior, or tramples on the rights and needs and feelings of others. With love, people come first. Thomas Merton says that love seeks one thing only: the good of the beloved. "If one were in a rapture like St. Paul," Meister Eckhart wrote, "and there was a sick man needing help, I think it would be best to throw off the rapture and show love by service to the needy."[14]

But where is such love to be found? When I look in myself I realize I have neither the equipment nor the personal qualities to fill a role like that. So I need the Holy Spirit. I need God coming into my heart and bringing his love and loving through me. I need *his* song, the song of the God of my life.

Let's put that into the pulpit and preach it. Let's tell that mother whose teen-age daughter has just moved in with a married man that God's music is still reverberating down the corridors of time. Let's tell that Christian whose brother has been picked up for dealing in drugs that the Troubadour is still singing the Ancient Star Song in the Plaza of Humanity.[15]

During World War II, I served as a chaplain in the U.S. Army Air Corps. My orders took me to the Aleutian islands shortly after the war ended, and there I found a disillusioned and bitter set of troops. I, too, became discouraged, for life "on the chain" (as we called the stormy islands) was not only difficult—it was miserable. To me the heavens became as brass, and reading the Bible a tedious exercise.

One day when Satan had seemingly done his worst and things were at their most abysmal, a recording arrived at the armed forces radio station on our island. It came from the "Old-Fashioned Revival Hour" broadcast in Long Beach, California. I played it through and heard a young man singing,

> I trust in God wherever I may be
>   upon the land or on the rolling sea,
> for come what may, from day to day,
>   my Heavenly Father watches over me.

> I trust in God, I know he cares for me
>   on mountain bleak or on the stormy sea;
> though billows roll, he keeps my soul,
>   my Heavenly Father watches over me.[16]

Doggerel, you might say. But the music found its way down through the accretions of my own sin and frustration and self-pity, through the layers of theology, ecclesiology, and military rank and protocol, until it reached my poor, shriveled heart. For the first time in weeks I knew, *I knew*, that God loved me, and cared for me, and was watching over me. Through the night of the Aleutian winter the Lord's song stayed with me, and I found as I sang those simple lines that I could pray again to the God of my life.

THE ANCIENT WAY

By now we know that the Psalmist was in a desperate situation. And I think we know what his prayer was: he wanted out, just as did the troops—and their chaplain—in the Aleutians.

But don't we all? Isn't that why people buy lottery tickets? Everyone would like to improve his situation. And why not? Suppose the Prodigal Son in Jesus' parable had decided not to get out of the pigsty, but to settle down and conduct experiments on the quality of life among pigs. Suppose that Christian, the leading character in *Pilgrim's Progress*, had decided not to struggle his way out of the Slough of Despond, but opted to stay there and take soil and water samples. There is a time to stay, but there is also a time to go. One of the Greek words for "time," *kairos*, is used in the New Testament to mean "high time," "the right time," "the fullness of time." That is God's time, when he is preparing the way for us to go.

Let's assume that you have a pretty fair idea that it is time for you to make your move. You sense that God has been communicating with you, telling you to go; but you are not sure which direction to take. You ask others what they think; you even ask me. What do I say? I say go to the Cross.

That may sound like lame advice, since it would appear you are a Christian and have already been to the Cross. But I am not talking about commitment; I am talking about grace and love and the Holy Spirit. I am talking about crucifixion of the self, so that the Holy Spirit can come into your life in a fresh way and give you direction and fuel. The direction is toward others; the fuel is love.

"I've been through that," you say. "I've made that trip. You don't understand my problem. I have to do something; should I do this or do that?"

I say with Jeremiah,

> Stand at the crossroads and look;
>   ask for the ancient paths,
> ask where the good way is, and walk in it,
>   and you will find rest for your souls."[17]

The good way, the ancient way, the way that Jesus walked, is the way of love. We have talked about what love is not. It's time to ask what love is.

Love is grace. A British soldier was relating to a preacher the gist of a sermon he had heard. The soldier said, "The minister told us that the grace of God is plentiful, sufficient for all need, and near at hand, but he did not tell us what the grace of God is. Perhaps, sir, you will be good enough to do that."[18]

I don't know what the preacher told him, but I know what grace is. It's more than forgiveness, more than unmerited favor. Grace is the love of God poured out, heaped up, pressed down, shaken together, and running over. Grace is the depth and wonder of the divine good pleasure, forbearance, and mercy. It is the decisive element in the saving work of God. It is love reaching out, drawing, embracing, redeeming, renewing, and building up the soul.

Love is sacrifice. The word is not popular in our current religious vocabulary, but it is quite familiar to love. Jesus Christ sacrificed his life on our behalf and in our stead. He did not have to do it. He did it for love. "Greater love has no one than this, that one lay down his life for his friends"[19]—that is, that one sacrifice his life for his friends. Love lays itself on the line, puts itself out, goes the second mile, the third mile, the fourth mile. Love never quits, or ever wants to quit.

You tell me there is a limit to what love can put up with? Then you are not walking in the ancient path, the good way; for love will put up with anything, undergo anything, endure anything, when God is directing it. The senseless things that happen to us threaten to drive us wild, but that is part of the sacrifice. "Though he slay me, yet will I hope in him."[20]

Love is the Holy Spirit. I don't understand why it took me so long to discover this truth. But after an experience on January 9, 1972, when I asked God to crucify me and to fill me with his Spirit, the whole universe seemed to fall into place and turn into a vessel of love.[21] I had not been exposed to some new teaching; I had read *The Calvary Road,* had studied the history of great revivals, and knew all the terminology—"stripping," "brokenness," "getting the self off the throne." But none of it had got down to the real me, to the bitterness in my soul.

Now the hard shell of the ego was cracked. As far as my life was concerned, the war was over. I became a pushover and wanted to love everybody. At a summer conference one of the women delegates who knew me remarked, "You're softer."

The Holy Spirit, I have learned, runs everything in the Christian life. He wrote the Bible; he inspired the church; he spread the Gospel; he drew the converts, and he is still doing it. Does God seem distant? Does Jesus seem to be a historical figure hard to relate to the computer age? Do you want to know which way to make your move? Ask the Holy Spirit. He is love, and love will tell you what to do. Love will make Jesus the Captain of your salvation—and will give you his song when the darkness falls.

CHAPTER EIGHT

Why Is This?

I say to God my Rock,
  "Why have you forgotten me?
Why must I go about mourning,
  oppressed by the enemy?
        —Psalm 42:9

THE REAL ENEMY

Imagine you are watching a live religious talk show on television. The screen shows a young woman, carefully made up, with masses of dark hair piled on her head, seated beside her host before the cameras. She is smiling and holds a Bible in her hands. The host beams at her, for he has been told she is about to relate an inspiring story of faith and trust. He says to her, "Now, Diane, share with the folks something of what God has done for you."

But instead of testifying, Diane begins to weep and to sob.

"Johnny," she says, "You won't believe this, but God has forgotten me. I go about mourning, oppressed by the enemy."

You sit there dumbfounded. Did this really happen? Would a Christian channel actually release such a testimony? And Johnny seems equally astonished. His eyes glaze, while the studio director faints.

All Diane did was recite the ninth verse of the Forty-second Psalm, which reflected her feelings as it has the feelings of millions of God's children. I created this bit of fantasy to show the difference between what the Bible actually is and what people think it is. Our Psalm was composed by a wounded spirit who, at the moment, was finding it hard to praise the Lord.

I confess to being weary of people who wear perpetual smiles to camouflage the situation. Rather than relax on a downy couch of unreal comfort, I prefer the granite slab of truth. If conditions have deteriorated, let's admit it and put it on the record. Let's neither deny it nor grovel in it.

The Psalmist is under such pressure that he says he can do nothing but go about mourning. What his problem is we do not know. He has an enemy who is vexing him, tormenting him, perhaps overwhelming him. Canvassing the scholars as they seek to identify this enemy can be a hilarious undertaking, for this is academic sport. One says the enemy is the murderous Queen Mother Athaliah. Another says it is Nebuchadnezzar of Babylon, another Ptolemy of Egypt, still another Antiochus Epiphanes, the Seleucid conqueror. Others vote for Absalom or Ahithophel.[1] Such guessing tells us nothing.

The New Testament gives us a true picture of an enemy who is more powerful than any military figure; who afflicts and oppresses everyone who believes in Jesus Christ; and against whom we, in our own strength, are helpless. Whether the Psalmist had this unseen enemy in mind is not clear, but I would say that Satan was perhaps a more accurate choice than Queen Mother Athaliah.

Satan is real. Demons are real. If the "Jesus People" of the 1960s did nothing else, they made Christians aware of the existence of this supernatural underworld. Demons are the true enemies of our souls. Of them we can say in the words of the Psalmist, "I hate them with perfect hatred: I count them mine enemies."[2] During that tempestuous decade, a number of young people on the West Coast who had been steeped in drugs became terrified by their meetings with demonic beings. (Christopher Pike, the surviving son of Bishop James Pike, explained to me, "No one can be on LSD for any time without encountering demons.")

In their desperation these young people turned to the only name they knew that had power over the agents of darkness. They called on Jesus without even knowing who he was, and Jesus delivered them. They became his followers; and that, I believe, is how the Jesus Movement was born.

Christians know that it is not Satan's usual policy to attack his own; he prefers to wait until a soul is clothed with Christ before he lays siege to it. To be oppressed by the enemy of our souls does not necessarily mean that a believer is subject to open assault as the drug freaks are. Satan's favorite battleground, if we but knew it, is the church pew. He passes nicely as a church member since he believes in God, believes the Bible, and knows Christ very well indeed.

In the church pew Satan begins to apply the pressure to the person beside him. "You say you're a Christian? You don't act like one. Take this morning at breakfast, for example. . . . You don't even believe like one. How much of the Bible can you really take? What are your honest thoughts about hell? . . . It seems odd for you to be posing as a solid member of this church when you know perfectly well there are a dozen other places you would rather be. Look around you. These people are all hypocrites and you know it. If you had any backbone you would walk out of here and never come back. After all, you have your integrity to think about. . . . That hymn you're singing—have you studied the words? How can you swallow them? 'Angels singing . . .realms of glory. . . Jesus loves you.' Balderdash."

And that's just the beginning.

But there is a way to meet such attacks. The King James rendition of Isaiah 59:19 reads, "When the enemy shall come in like a flood, the Spirit of the Lord shall lift up a standard against him." We are no match for the devil, but Jesus is; and in the name of Jesus we can say, "Satan, you are a liar. I do believe. I do love God's people. I reject your accusings. God has consigned you to hell. Go back where you belong."

SOMETHING LOOSE

There is a conspiracy, we are well aware, to destroy the human race. We are familiar with the tactics used: suspicion, discord, arguments, controversies, malice, vengeance, hatred, pride, fear, lust, greed, and the rest. But for overall strategy Satan is more subtle; his aim is simply to convince people that God has forgotten them.

When the Psalmist asks his God, "Why have you forgotten me?" he has broken past the simple fact of evil and is grappling with the master strategist of the invisible underworld. The question does not mean that the Psalmist is convinced he has been forgotten of God. The issue is in doubt, and the question has been put. The same question is asked in the memorable prayer that opens Psalm 22, "My God, my God, why have you forsaken me?"—a prayer that Jesus repeated on the cross.

The very fact that the question is raised in the form of a prayer is proof that the existence of God is assumed. And since it was raised in both the Old and New Testaments, it is no sacrilege when a believer today is puzzled or bewildered. Charles Spurgeon says, "If the Lord be indeed our refuge, when we find no refuge, it is time to be raising the question, 'Why is this?' "[3]

Within our evangelical communion, thousands of earnest lovers of Christ are asking the same question: "Why is this?" We became evangelicals because we wanted God. We did not seek the sudden popularity that has overtaken our "movement." For decades we were derided and ignored and branded the "Protestant underworld." Now suddenly we are welcomed to the highest councils of government; politicians curry our favor; we are seated at public functions. We have become "chic."

But what does it all mean without God? We thought we had

settled it once and for all on our knees. We thought that God was on our side, but now we're not all that sure. It seems God is taking his time with us. We thought we made a commitment. We "gave our all to Jesus." What more does he expect?

Tozer declares, "The whole transaction of religious conversion has been made mechanical and spiritless. Faith may now be exercised without a jar to the moral life and without embarrassment to the Adamic ego. Christ may be 'received' without creating any special love for him in the soul of the receiver. The man is 'saved,' but he is not hungry nor thirsty after God. He is specifically taught to be satisfied and encouraged to be content with little."[4]

Richard Quebedeaux reports that "some evangelicals" are not only divorcing and remarrying, they are drinking, smoking, swearing, telling lewd jokes, dancing to rock music, using marijuana, gambling, reading porno books, engaging in homosexual and other unnatural sex acts—as well as challenging parts of the Bible![5]

Where do we go? In the words of Job:

"If only I knew where to find him;
   if only I could go to his dwelling! . . .
But if I go to the east, he is not there;
   if I go to the west, I do not find him.
When he is at work in the north, I do not see him;
   when he turns to the south, I catch no glimpse of him."[6]

If we seek God in his own house, we may find that Satan's tactics have taken over, with the result that the church leaders are at sixes and sevens. Or possibly we find a hyperactive church and are in danger of being trampled. Give me a live church every time, but I'll admit it takes a drop-forge constitution to stay with some of our church programs. If we look for fellow-seekers in the prayer meeting, we may find that the prayers have been trimmed and the meeting turned into a Bible lecture. There's nothing wrong with a good Bible lecture—except when it takes the place of prayer.

If we stay home and turn on the "electric church," we may be richly blessed by a Gospel message, or we may be exposed to stagy musical productions, hard-sell promotions, giveaways, telethons, rampant heterodoxy, theological eyewash, instant religion, saccharine pap, wriggling entertainment, dubious healings, megalomania, and noise.

If we rush out the door, fleeing from man-made religious contrivings, and take our search for God to some quiet natural scene, we may be no better off. Without withdrawing into prudery, we may be appalled by the human sights that present themselves at the seashore. If we prefer the lake, we stand a chance of being deafened by gasoline motors. And if we pull on our boots and take to a mountain trail, we may flush out a drug cult in the canyons.

If we choose to mingle with the poor whom Jesus loved and seek to find God by meeting human need, we may succeed. Many a faithful servant of God, an unsung Mother Teresa, has discovered God's presence among the wretched ones. The Bible tells us he is always there. He is with the boat people, the street people, the left-out people, the transients, the victims of fire and flood and famine, the very old and very young, the disfranchised and disadvantaged.

Yet in North America we find that the poor who seem so close to God are not always served by godly spokesman. Continuous uproar in the public media suggests that some are less interested in impressing the Almighty than they are in facing-off the welfare board, the urban renewal board, the parole board, or some other government agency. Divine assistance is not in the same league with federal funding; prayer does not carry the same clout as bannering and protesting.

What can the seeker after God do? He has a real sense of being forgotten. He senses a satanic element in the environment, something loose in the world and in the church that is not of God. The Psalmist was aware of it too. Jesus felt it in the desert and at Golgotha. Paul felt it at Ephesus. Luther felt it at the Wartburg. The Jews felt it at Auschwitz. The German pastors felt it at Barmen. We all felt it while viewing the Jonestown tragedy.

We cannot isolate it or define it, but it is oppressing us and keeping us from God. Has he really forgotten us? Is Satan in charge?

GOD MY ROCK

But wait. What about the expression the Psalmist uses in this verse, "God my Rock"? Is there anything in that? Yes, a great deal. God is compared with a rock all through Scripture, and many times he is directly called "Rock."

The Lord is my rock, my fortress and my deliverer;
  my God is my rock, in whom I take refuge. . . .
For who is God besides the Lord?
  And who is the Rock except our God? . . .
The Lord lives! Praise be to my Rock!

May the words of my mouth and the meditation of my heart
  be pleasing in your sight,
O Lord, my Rock and my Redeemer.

He will hide me in the shelter of his tabernacle
  and set me high upon a rock.
Then my head will be exalted
  above the enemies who surround me.

To you I call, O Lord my Rock;
  do not turn a deaf ear to me.

Lead me to the rock that is higher than I.

Come, let us sing for joy to the Lord;
  let us shout aloud to the Rock of our salvation.[7]

The same imagery is carried through the New Testament—

Everyone who hears these words of mine and puts them into practice is like a wise man who built his house on the rock.[8]

Our forefathers . . . all ate the same spiritual food and drank from the spiritual rock that accompanied them, and that rock was Christ.[9]

—and has come down in song to our own day:

"Oh, safe to the Rock that is higher than I. . . ."
"Rock of Ages, cleft for me. . . ."
"Jesus is a Rock in a weary land. . . ."

When I think of a rock, I picture a mighty monolith like Gibraltar, or Ayers Rock in Australia, or Ship Rock in New Mexico, or another Ship Rock I knew in the Aleutians. Battered by storms for thousands of years, they remain stalwart and unmovable against the skyline. Regardless of what happens, they are *there*.

We in our flustered lives can mourn and lament, we can sway back and forth under the fierce assaults of the oppressor until we are nearly flattened, we can complain that God has forgotten us, but the Rock remains. The Psalmist knew that. He knew that he was not in fact forgotten. He knew that truth eventually would triumph over the forces of evil and all would come out right in the end. That's what it means to believe in God.

We can say the same. No matter how threateningly the gates of hell may yawn before us, Jesus has told us that they would never prevail against his church. To us who believe, God is still the Sovereign Lord and Father of Jesus Christ, no matter what our circumstances at the moment. His purpose is inexorable, his truth indestructible. His Spirit is still in the world, thwarting Satan and pouring out healing love into human hearts.

The Lord lives! Praise be to my Rock, my shelter from the stormy blast and my eternal home.

CHAPTER NINE

Taunts

My bones suffer mortal agony
as my foes taunt me,
saying to me all day long,
'Where is your God?' "
—Psalm 42:10

THE GARLAND OF SUFFERING

Wo Li, a hoarder of sugar in the People's Republic of China, is arrested by the secret police and dragged from his home to the village square, where he is placed on trial before a "people's court." He is ashamed.

Four-year-old Reginald, strolling with his parents through the state fairground, suddenly demands a cotton-candy cone. His parents say No and jerk him past the crowded concession into the midway. Reginald throws a tantrum to embarrass them, rolling on the ground, kicking and screaming. Bystanders pause and laugh. The parents smart with shame.

Bixley Armbruster, bond broker and reputable citizen, arrives home from the office one evening to be greeted by his wife and daughter in tears. They have been watching the news, which reported his indictment by a grand jury on fraud charges. Bixley's shame is overwhelming.

What emotion ranks lower than shame? Cruel shame that makes the skin crawl? Surely nothing in human experience can match it. To be found out, to be exposed to the pitiless sneer, to learn what people are saying—this kind of shame is the deepest agony of all. We can take pain and loss and illness and tragedy with a show of bravery; but shame and disgrace are different. No one wants to be derided or held up to public scorn. We say, anything but that! God preserve us from the plight of the author of Psalm 69:

> Shame covers my face.
> I am a stranger to my brothers,
>   an alien to my own mother's sons. . . .
> Scorn has broken my heart
>   and has left me helpless;
> I looked for sympathy, but there was none,
>   for comforters, but I found none.[1]

Of all the sufferings of our Lord Jesus Christ, the most affecting to us and perhaps the hardest for him to endure, apart from the shadow across his Father's face, was the jeering of the crowds. "He trusts in God," they said. "Let God rescue him now if he wants him."[2] As he hung on the cross, Jesus may have recalled the prophetic words of the Psalmist: "My bones suffer mortal agony as my foes taunt me."

The reproach that fell on the Psalmist, as well as on our Lord and on the early Christians, has not fallen on many of us. North Americans live in an enlightened pluralistic society. Religion has achieved respectability; church activities are protected by law. We happily wear our Praise-the-Lord T-shirts and Jesus buttons in the shopping malls, and slap bumper stickers on our cars that read, "In case of rapture this car will be unmanned."

Well, now. Does it mean that all those arrests and trials and massacres in the name of religion that marked the centuries before our own have passed into oblivion? Hardly. In many overseas regions today God's people are taunted for their faith, and there is no reason to believe that the situation will improve. An unimpeachable source tells us the night is coming when no man can work.

"Suffering is of the essence of the mission of the Messiah," writes R. J. Hammer.[3] He refers to Mark 8:31, which describes how Jesus "then began to teach them that the Son of Man must suffer many things and be rejected by the elders, chief priests and teachers of the law, and that he must be killed and after three days rise again." But as a follower of the Messiah, I must say suffering does not seem to be my mission at the moment, even though that may change at the next traffic light.

It isn't that I dread any thought of pain, or that God isn't ready to sustain me. I am thirsting for God, just as you are, and if the quest calls for suffering, that should be "it." Miguel de Molinos was probably right when he wrote, "You are never at any time nearer to God than when under tribulation."[4] But when Peter says that we are to "rejoice" when we participate in the sufferings of Christ, he has moved off my turf. What I have had to undergo for my faith has not been all that significant. Such talk seems a far cry from my weekly visits to God's house, where everyone is welcomed by smiling ushers and treated to a good biblical sermon and a pleasing anthem.

In my younger days as a new Christian I wanted to prove myself a hero for Christ. I would gladly (so I imagined) have exchanged places with John Hus, put on the inquisitor's dunce cap and clown suit, and died in flames for my faith. Today I wonder about it. Romantic thoughts of valor have a way of evaporating when one becomes, as the Psalmist puts it, "the song of the drunkards." Just how much mockery—not to say torture—could my eager, youthful zeal have endured? Even today I am reluctant to say with Rutherford, "I take his cross in my arms with joy; I bless it, I rejoice in it. Suffering for Christ is my garland."[5]

In any case, right now no one is asking me to suffer. I

haven't even been asked to increase my pledge. Certainly no one is urging me, as Paul urged Timothy, to join him "in suffering for the Gospel." Given the circles in which I move, I hardly know what's involved in suffering for the Gospel. I'll be glad to send a check, and the mail brings requests enough. But suffer shame? My bones in mortal agony? For Jesus?

It all sounds strange.

SQUEEZING GOOD OUT OF BAD

This is not a book about suffering, but a book about human beings in search of God. Yet our two Psalms say much about suffering, as do all the Psalms. Many a person in pain or in agony of spirit has found relief and comfort in the words of the Psalmist. Probably no other writings have so spoken to humans in distress.

The New Testament approaches suffering from a different perspective. Frank Uttley tells us there are two kinds of suffering in the New Testament, one being persecution, the other invalidism due to sickness and disease. Jesus, he says, commended the one and cured the other.[6]

The eighth Beatitude reads, "Blessed are those who are persecuted because of righteousness."[7] Jesus added, "If they persecuted me, they will persecute you also."[8] The word *persecute* comes from the Latin *per* with *sequi*, meaning "to follow or go after someone." The same meaning attaches to the Greek New Testament word *dioko*. It's hard for Western democracies to relate to such a word, since our one certain guarantee above all others is freedom of religion.

Minority groups in North America understand the word *persecute* better than the rest of us. What they have suffered defies description. As late as World War II, when I was a chaplain serving segregated troops at Hamilton Field, California, a young black returnee from the South Pacific combat zone told me what it was like for one of his race to have a weekend pass in "color-blind" Honolulu: "In town we were permitted to do just three things: we could go to a movie or sit in the park or go to church."

But even going to church may be made "off-limits" if, as

many Christians believe, a new wave of religious persecution is coming. And it won't be just for minorities. If the prospect sounds far-fetched, I suggest you try negotiating for property to start a city church and see what kind of resistance you meet.

Will persecution for the name of Jesus necessarily be a bad thing? It will hurt, yes; but it may bring the revival we have needed for so long. It wouldn't be the first time God has squeezed good out of bad.

The first recorded revival in Scripture came to Israel when the little nation faced annihilation. The Philistines were threatening to attack when Samuel summoned the people to meet him at Mizpah where, he said, "I will intercede with the Lord for you." Samuel commanded the Israelites to put away their false gods and to fast and repent. They did. The record states, "He [Samuel] cried out to the Lord on Israel's behalf, and the Lord answered him."[9] The people were saved, and the nation was renewed.

The eighteenth-century evangelical revival in England and Scotland under the Wesleys and Whitefield came during a time of intense national privation and suffering. The sudden transformation of Britain into an industrial giant created both great wealth and abject misery. The working classes were uprooted. Children were forced into the mines and factories. And it was precisely among these people, the lower classes, that the revival took hold.

Simultaneously the Great Awakening broke out in the American colonies. While it affected the churches in Boston and Philadelphia, it also evoked strong resistance; the entire Harvard College faculty issued a rebuke to the evangelist George Whitefield. But the rural areas proved fertile soil, for the people were undergoing great hardship, struggling to carve a civilized society out of hostile wilderness. The Bible became the most-read book from New England to Georgia, and churches sprang up everywhere.

When revival came again in 1858, it was a time of severe economic instability in America. Banks failed everywhere. The wealthy found themselves paupers. Bankruptcies, frauds, and defaults turned the nation into a state of panic. Industry's hearth fires went out; wheels stood still. Just at that time a prayer meeting was started on the third floor of a building on Fulton Street, New York City. Four men showed up. Within an astonishingly short time it had spread to other cities and literally to the entire nation. A million members were added to the churches.

Today the churches of East Berlin are suffering the oppression of a disapproving and unfriendly government. The spiritual life is strong. In West Berlin, where the churches are free, it has been estimated that only one percent of the population attends services on Sunday morning.

The strongest evangelical church in Asia is in South Korea, and its most fervent disciples for the past thirty years have been the refugees who streamed southward at the close of World War II, when Communist forces invaded North Korea. Five hundred North Korean pastors were shot through the back of the head during that invasion. Today all over South Korea thousands of Christians are flocking to the churches each day for prayer at five o'clock—in the morning. To attend one of those meetings is an unforgettable experience.

Our excursion into history should teach us one thing: a lot of our current discussion of "revival" in the church is superficial. Spiritual awakening does not normally come to the prosperous and affluent. Revival is born out of tribulation, defeat, and straitened circumstances, when people don't know which way to turn, so they turn to God.

THE MUSIC OF PERSECUTION

In our Psalm the suffering goes on, verse after verse: "My bones suffer mortal agony." The original wording is that the Psalmist's bones are "crushed," as by a wall that is knocked down. Why "bones"? If they are not actually broken (and the pain of a fracture can be excruciating), then the plucking and stripping of his good name, the ridiculing of his faith, may be having a psychosomatic effect. He feels the pain not just in his soul, not even in his nervous system, but in his bones.

Is it any wonder that this Psalm and others like it have found their way into the marrow of the human race? As the

Psalmist sings his lament he takes along millions of people who can identify with him each step of the way.

It might be worthwhile to review what makes the Book of Psalms different from other literature. There are plenty of sad songs lying about to choose from, in hundreds of languages, all dwelling on the plight of the one composing. Perhaps the Psalms are unique only in their thirst for God. They do not limit their scope to a grief stricken wail, to a "Mayday" or "S.O.S." entreaty. The Psalmist wants more. He yearns for God himself, the living God, that he might rest his soul in the Beloved. And he yearns for his people, that they too might be delivered.

Ambrose, the fourth-century bishop of Milan, once wrote, "This is the peculiarity of the Psalter, that everyone can use its words as if they were completely and individually his own. When other passages of Scripture are used in church, the words are drowned in the noise of talking. But when the Psalter is read, all are dumb."[10]

In the long saga of religious belief, the Psalms have comforted Christians who were suffering torture and death at the hands of pagans. They have comforted Jews in the hands of Christians, French Huguenots and Scottish Covenanters in the hands of Roman Catholics, Catholics in the hands of Protestants, Puritans in the hands of Anglicans, Quakers in the hands of Puritans, missionaries in the hands of cannibals, Armenians in the hands of Turks, American flyers in the hands of North Vietnamese.

Our Lord Jesus Christ suffered on the cross and died with a Psalm on his lips. So did the first Christian martyr, Stephen. When Paul and Silas found themselves chained in a jail in Philippi, unable to sleep because their backs were sore from the whippings, they encouraged themselves by singing Psalms. Young Christians like Perpetua and Felicitas, facing lions and other wild beasts in the Roman amphitheaters, went to meet them boldly speaking or singing the words of a Psalm.[11]

Over the bloody centuries hundreds of thousands of condemned men, women, and children have met violent death with a Psalm on their lips. James Guthrie, minister of the Gospel, was led out of Edinburgh's Tolbooth prison to his place of execution in 1661 for refusing to recognize the king's authority over the church. As he stood on the scaffold he proclaimed the words of Psalm 118:24, "This is the day which the Lord hath made; we will rejoice and be glad in it." Daniel McMichael, led into the fields outside London in 1685 to be shot for his denial of the papacy, died singing our Forty-second Psalm.

Describing the faith of the Huguenots, Florimond de Ré-mond called them "the pick of the [French] nation." "Their men," he said, "habitually deny themselves, seemed struck by the Holy Spirit. They loved the Bible or the singing of spiritual songs and psalms better than dances or hautboys." As for the women, people saw "young virgins go to the scaffold as gaily as they would go to the bridal couch, crying only on Christ their Savior, or singing a Psalm."[12]

So it has been with sufferers for three thousand years. People of all races and stations in life—tradesmen, charwomen, fieldhands, factory workers, poets, musicians, scholars, scientists, rulers, businessmen, churchmen, housewives, students, public servants—have been guided, elevated, consoled, and inspired by the Psalms.

But the tribulations of others don't seem to move us all that much. They may even comfort us in an odd way, for misery loves company; and our generation has known misery. We may not all suffer pangs of hunger, but we have an impressive modern-day collection of illnesses. In some areas nearly half our children are growing up in broken homes, and they know what pain is. Some of our psychological sufferings may be more acute than those of the ancient martyrs—or so they seem to us.

What are we to conclude? That our suffering will lead us to God? Did the Psalmist find the help he wanted in the midst of his trials? And will God make that same kind of help available to us? At least we can ask. Martyn Lloyd-Jones once said that the whole art of the Christian life is the art of asking questions.[13]

CHAPTER TEN

Cruelty and Deceit

Vindicate me, O God,
and plead my cause against an ungodly nation;
rescue me from deceitful and wicked men.
—Psalm 43:1

ARE THE LIGHTS ON?

Now the issue is joined. These words of our Psalm mean that you and I cannot stand dawdling on the periphery any longer; we must plunge into the center. God's moral character is at stake. What kind of God is God? Is he a just God? Is he kind? Does he love the human race? Or is he some kind of uncaused Cause or unmoved Mover? Did he wind up the

For the discussion of Psalm 42:11, see note on page 47.

universe to let it run down, or did he bring a Hebrew slave tribe out of Egypt?

Does he, as the prophets affirmed, care about the poor and needy, the widow and orphan? Did he send his Son to us on that first Christmas day? And his Holy Spirit at Pentecost?

It's such a struggle to think of God, to imagine what he's like. The author of *The Cloud of Unknowing* tells me, in fact, that I cannot think of God. "He may be well loved, but he may not be thought of."[1] If such be the case, I shall tax my brain no further. For years I have loved God with all my heart, but love is not the immediate issue. What I want to know is, *Is everything all right?* Not between me and God, but with God himself? Is he God, is he on the throne, is he in charge of reality? The Psalmist wants God to vindicate him but even more, he wants God to vindicate himself. And so do I.

You and I have been taught that God created everything for love, but something happened. Evil entered the environment. It has been variously described, sometimes as a fallen angel, or a swerve of the atoms, or a black pall suspended over the earth, or a lump of mud thrown into a clear running stream, or an uproar among the gods, or a flaw or defect in humanity. Man has been called neither good nor evil, but "a good thing spoiled."

The one unimpeachable authority on all this is the Bible. It tells us that the one true God made man in his own image, but that man was corrupted by sin and the image was tarnished and broken. In revealing this truth it vindicates the character of God.

When we approach the Bible as a true scientist approaches a natural object—humbly, with a desire to let it teach him—we will learn that God is not only truth, but also beauty and goodness and above all love. We will learn that rightness and wrongness characterize the universe—only temporarily! Some day the glory of God will cover the earth as the waters cover the sea; meanwhile, God stands on the side of rightness.

Seen from the divine perspective as the Bible interprets it, life makes sense. Whether we like it or not, God's values and standards govern us.

Dag Hammarskjöld, the first secretary general of the United Nations, was convinced for years that life did *not* make sense. He wrote, "What I ask for is unreasonable: that life shall have a meaning. What I strive for is impossible: that my life shall acquire a meaning." But Hammarskjöld changed. He wrote later that he found the meaning of his life in God: "The time came when the beliefs in which I was once brought up and which, in fact, had given my life direction even while my intellect still challenged their validity, were recognized by me as mine in their own right and by my free choice."[2]

Archibald MacLeish wrote the drama *J.B.* in an effort to discern the meaning of life by analyzing the character of God. The effort fails as the brutal realities of human existence are rehearsed.

> Millions and millions of mankind
> Burned, crushed, broken, mutilated,
> Slaughtered, and for what? For thinking!
> For walking round the world in the wrong
> Skin, the wrong-shaped noses, eyelids:
> Sleeping the wrong night wrong city—
> London, Dresden, Hiroshima.

The play concludes that God explains nothing and might best be ignored.

> Blow on the coal of the heart, my darling. . . .
> It's all the light now.
> Blow on the coal of the heart.
> The candles in churches are out.
> The lights have gone out in the sky. . . .[3]

"Vindicate me against such blasphemy, O God!" cries the Psalmist. "Champion me. Justify me. Stand up for me. Defend and support me!" As a human individual under attack, he is struggling with the problem of his own faith. The situation appears rigged. But he wants more than reassurance or even clearance; he wants the Lord to take the initiative. All through the Forty-second Psalm his prayer has been a description rather than a plea. Now in the Forty-third he is on praying ground, supplicating, petitioning, beseeching.

The story is told of a minister of the old school who was issuing from the pulpit a long, sonorous prayer extolling the virtues and perfections of God. Several minutes passed without a break in the flow, whereupon a little lady in the front pew hissed, "Ask him for something!"

The Psalmist is now asking for something. He wants God to plead his cause, and you and I can echo his cry. "Lord, do something! Prove that the lights have not gone out! Turn them on! Let your roar be heard out of Zion. Tell the world that the gates of hell shall not prevail against your church. Reveal yourself for what you are. Show that our faith in you is based on actuality!"

Oh, what we would give to see God bare his arm; to see him once and for all stop the mouths of those who keep referring to him as a myth, or a relic of childhood, or an invention of priestcraft to oppress the masses and drug them into submission! But that is not the way God works; or at least, as we shall see, it is not the way he works today.

THE CUP OF DEMONS

"Plead my cause against a merciless people; rescue me from deceitful and wicked men." Deceit and cruelty. Abuse and treachery. People today tend to call them by other names: sadism, paranoia, megalomania, double-agent espionage, revolutionary codes. The behavior is the same; such terms do not describe, they attempt to justify. But Dachau is still Dachau, and Jonestown Jonestown. A swindler is still a swindler, and a battered wife a battered wife.

The Psalmist asks his God to rescue him from lying men. Maurice Samuel, in his discussion with Mark Van Doren, has pointed out that the Psalms generally treat the lie as the first foundation of evil-doing.[4] Psalm 15 praises the man "who keeps his oath even when it hurts." Psalm 34, attributed to David, reads:

> Whoever of you loves life
>   and desires to see many good days,
> keep your tongue from evil,
>   and your lips from speaking lies.[5]

And Psalm 24, also of David, asks:

> Who may ascend the hill of the Lord?
> Who may stand in his holy place?
> He who has clean hands and a pure heart,
> who does not lift up his soul to an idol
> or swear by what is false.[6]

As the master of deceit, Satan is a liar and the father of lies. We cannot speak of deceitful and wicked persons without speaking of him, for he is the ruler of this age.[7] When Christians lapse into speaking lies and swearing by what is false, they are in Peter's words "denying the sovereign Lord who bought them."[8] Paul warned the Corinthians that they could not drink of the cup of the Lord and the cup of demons too.[9] In other words, we cannot at the same time be filled with lies and filled with Truth.

The Book of Revelation reserves a special place of judgment in the second death for all liars.[10] The Sixty-second Psalm declares that "the highborn are but a lie."[11] What would you say about the current scene? If we are honest we will have to admit that lying is still a way of life today, particularly when people find themselves in embarrassing or awkward circumstances.

"I had no idea the gun was loaded."

"All engines were shut down before we went off shift."

"The roof was in perfect condition when we sold the house."

"The order was filled exactly as it was written out."

"We just drove around town and talked until four this morning."

"I was watching the speedometer and was doing exactly fifty-five miles an hour."

"Our dog never left the yard all day."

"You understand our failure to report this discrepancy was simply a clerical error."

"It was completely his fault."

Lying is all too common a practice on the witness stand. It is the language of convenience not only in the courtroom, but in the board room, the market place, the school, the hospital, the newsroom, even the church. If nailed, the lie is extenuated. It is passed off as political rhetoric, extravagant or imaginative language, technical jargon, exaggeration, misquotation, expediency, satire, double-talk, phobic reaction, diplomatic terminology, situation ethic, "inoperative statement," or mental lapse.

Lying can destroy a nation. America might still be in the agonies of Watergate if certain individuals had not decided to stop lying and start telling the truth.

How does one rescue his life from the slime pit of deceit? How does he avoid using guile as people use knives and forks, to satisfy their own desires? How does he escape the snare of his own basic dishonesty and walk out under the sky and lift up his hands for the truth?

I remember Reinhold Niebuhr once telling the students at the University of California in Berkeley, "The solution to history is that there is no solution." He was right. Within history as we know it there are no human answers. There is no rescue, no way out. With men it is impossible. We are stuck with merciless people, with deceitful and wicked men.

But suppose there was One who came from beyond space and time, and shared our lot, and was betrayed by deceitful persons and put to death by cruel persons. Suppose he was the embodiment of all that we sought to find on earth but failed to find. And then suppose that after his death his body could not be found, and that his followers remembered that he had said he would rise again from the grave, and would send them an Advocate, a Counselor, who would be the Spirit of Truth. *And what we could not do, this Person would do in us and through us and for us.*

Do you think that would help?

ENDS AND MEANS

The message of the New Testament is that if we cannot keep our tongue from evil and our lips from speaking lies, there is One who can. That One is the Holy Spirit whom Jesus sent. He is the Advocate who comes alongside and pleads our cause—exactly what the Psalmist was asking for.

For a number of years I unconsciously avoided the subject of the Holy Spirit. That was a mistake. Yet I was not alone; it seems to me that the Spirit's ministry, for one reason or another, is not always appreciated or understood in many of our churches.

During many years I spent in the active ministry, the Holy Spirit's name passed my reverent lips every day, yet I cannot say that I really knew him. Formally I honored and worshiped him, but informally we just weren't close. I never imagined we could be. Even though I called him "He," a Person, I still thought of him as "it," an effect or influence. I did not apprehend his crucial importance to every phase and aspect of Christian living.

Now he has taken charge of my life and I have handed over the keys. I still don't know much about him, but we have a family intimacy. Reverence remains, but the formalism is gone. Hearing his name sends a quickening of love through me and gives my heart the kind of flutter it has had for years upon hearing the name of Jesus.

How had I failed to grasp the Spirit's importance to the life of the believer? I think I know my original mistake: it was to make the Holy Spirit the caboose on the Gospel train. He became a theological benediction of sorts, a kind of throat-clearing at the end of a pulpit sentence. When I mentioned his name it was to give ballast to a point and profundity to the whole discourse.

The Holy Spirit does not appreciate such a role. If he cannot be sovereign he prefers to leave; and so he quietly slips out, taking his gifts with him. Now, when the Living Water ceases to flow, the church usually looks for a stuck valve in its machinery. But the problem just is not there. Jacking up the program or polishing the image will not help. We're talking about departed glory! I sometimes wonder, if the church had a Missing Persons file, whether the Holy Spirit would not be the first name on the list.

Jesus said that when the Spirit did come, he would "convict the world of guilt in regard to sin and righteousness and judgment."[12] We turn on the six o'clock news and what comes over? Cruelty and deceit, hate and vengeance. Because the Holy Spirit is love, he will not put up with it. He will not countenance the violent or vengeful spirit. He will not endorse the terrorist who, after deluding himself into thinking he is engaged in "the people's cause," plants a bomb under a bus seat. He will not bless the theologian who thinks he is aiding the downtrodden by advocating "Christian violence." Better to suffer for doing good, says Peter, than for doing evil.[13] " 'Not by might or by power, but by my Spirit,' says the Lord."[14]

We can, and often do, attempt to achieve good through evil, but the end does not justify the means. The Holy Spirit does not join such human conspirings. If he does not thwart them, it is because he intends to fulfill the divine purpose in some other way—perhaps at the Day of Judgment.

To grapple philosophically with the problem of evil is not my intent, even if I could. I am simply asking how the Spirit of God goes about convicting people of their sins. Take for example the modern-day tax-cheater, price-fixer, or political grafter. Or take the hijacker, bomber, sniper, or torturer. What if anything will change him? What will sensitize his conscience, make him stop defending himself, bring about his confession and admission of guilt, fill him with remorse and a desire to make restitution? What will cause him, as it were, to rejoin the human race?

The answer is the Word of God faithfully proclaimed. The Scripture is the sword of the Spirit to pierce people's hearts. The Holy Spirit uses the text to convict the world of its guilt. And yet that is only part of his ministry. He also leads the seeker into truth, glorifies Jesus Christ, and brings to the church's remembrance his words of love. The Holy Spirit is love, and his mission is not to condemn but to save, just as Jesus' was and is.

There is a judgment and there is a hell, but the word of the Gospel is not wrath; it is love. There is no other way to be saved but by love.

It's worth noting that our Psalmist wanted to be rescued from merciless, deceitful, and wicked men, but he did not demand revenge upon his enemies. He could have used a thunderstorm, as at Mizpah, or an interruption in the earth's orbit, as at Aijalon.[15] But he knew well enough what modern man cannot seem to learn, that no activity of human beings is so empty in its results, so self-defeating, and so deadly in its ultimate effect on the soul as vengeance.

The New Testament tells us what to do with enemies. It tells us to love them, and they will melt like the frost before the warm sunshine. When Sadat went to Tel Aviv, Egyptian bunting suddenly appeared in the streets. That is God's way. We were not given this earth to destroy it by our furious quarrels. Earth was a love gift from the heavenly Father; we are supposed to take care of it.

As Christians we love the sinner and hate the sin, we love the arsonist and hate his torch. And if we are sincere about it, who knows? Perhaps the Spirit of God will suffuse our equivocating, vacillating lives with a touch—just the barest touch—of the Father's power and glory.

The Holy Spirit has a good many things to impart to you and me. Some of them we can absorb now, some after we are wiser in the faith, and some will wait (as Paul says) until perfection comes. And what a day that will be! When we sit down at the banquet table of the Messiah, it will not be to a TV dinner.

CHAPTER ELEVEN
The Fortress

You are God my *Fortress.*
Why have you rejected me?
Why must I go about mourning,
oppressed by the enemy?
—Psalm 43:2

THE NARROW BEACH

The truth of God is not an advancing armored column, invading new territory and conquering as it goes.

It is not a drilling operation, quarrying hidden treasure from the hills or dredging it from the ocean floor.

Nor is it a spaceship piercing the black holes of the universe and sending back signals that will help solve the interstellar mysteries.

Nor is it yet a scrambling quarterback, rolling out to pass, looking for options, and adapting his plan to rapidly changing maneuvers on the playing field.

The truth of God is none of these. Rather, says the Psalmist, it is a fortress, a command post established on a Rock.[1] Truth is a bastion, and bastions don't fluctuate. *Ein' feste Burg ist unser Gott.* "A Mighty Fortress Is Our God." Amid the swirling tides of relativism, in the face of the Lilliputian assaults of men, the fortress remains steadfast and impregnable in its own defense.

And where are you and I? Right now we are standing with the Psalmist, barefoot on the narrow beach below the fortress. We have no ammunition, no climbing gear, no map, no alternatives or contingency plans, and no idea what to do next. If there is an entrance, we don't know where it is. Everything appears snug, tight, and grim.

"You are God my fortress. Why have you rejected me?" We stare at the gray eminence before us, those steep, unassailable cliffs, and we wonder frankly whether it is worth trying to know God. Perhaps he will always be veiled in clouds and mist, the Great Unapproachable, the Totally Other. Herbert Spencer said that the one sure thing we know about God is that he is unknowable.[2] Job put it bluntly:

> "Why do you hide your face
> and consider me your enemy?"[3]

The Psalmist himself is expressing the same feeling. If God is in the fortress, he says in Psalm 44, perhaps he is sleeping.

> Awake, O Lord! Why do you sleep?
> Rouse yourself! Do not reject us forever.

> Why do you hide your face
> and forget our misery and oppression?[4]

And in Psalm 88 he continues the thought.

> Why, O Lord, do you reject me
> and hide your face from me?
>
> From my youth I have been afflicted and close to death;
> I have suffered your terrors and am in despair.
> Your wrath has swept over me;
> your terrors have destroyed me.
> All day long they surround me like a flood;
> they have completely engulfed me.
> You have taken my companions and loved ones from me;
> the darkness is my closest friend.[5]

But perhaps we should not pay too much attention to the Psalmist. We might say, "Let him alone; he is always complaining. You and I can do something about this problem. Why should we be trapped on this beach, barefoot, with no climbing tools? Let's get to a sport shop and pick up an outfit. If people can make it up the face of the Eigerwand and El Capitan, we ought to be able to lick this thing. A bit of nylon rope, and a few pitons in the side of that wall, and it won't look so invincible."

Unfortunately that way is disaster. The beach is littered with the rubble of those who have tried to scale the heights to God. They have put up every kind of religious scaffolding— vigils, fasts, diets, prayers, beatings, incantations, temples, mausoleums, pilgrimages—but the distance between the ordinary human being and his Maker remains as vast as ever.

So here we are. If we aren't rejected, it looks as if we are, it feels as if we are, and what's the difference? We read our Bibles dutifully. We go to church on Sundays. We pray after a fashion and even tell people we are saved, but when something happens to us (as it happened to the Psalmist) we feel just as far away from God as ever. That's why we thirst. If only we could see him and talk with him face to face as Abraham did, and as Moses did . . .

Look again at that cliff. See if you can find any cracks, any footholds, any chimneys. You will notice that the day is wearing on; night is approaching, and the wind is rising, and so is the tide. It doesn't appear as if we can stay much longer where we are. But where can we go? If we choose to go nowhere and do nothing, we are in worse shape than ever.

Is this the way our thirst for God must end—by drowning? Perhaps if we beat against the cliff it will relieve our frustration. Or perhaps we should just shake our fists and shout our defiance—and forget the whole thing and toss in the sponge and call it quits and give up and curse God and die.

THE VIRTUE OF ADVERSITY

But it seems there is a better way. There is an answer to the Psalmist's question, "Why have you rejected me?" It is found, not in the Psalms, but at the back of the Book. When we turn to the New Testament we find that we are down on the beach for a good reason: to acquire discipline. Discipling means discipline, and hardship is simply one component of Christian training.

If we are thirsting for the living God, there is a regimen to undergo. It is not a course in rock-climbing, nor is it the accumulation of points; rather it is a series of exercises and tough disciplines that will build our trust. Progress will be measured, not by the clock or the pulse rate, but by our willingness to lay hold of God in the teeth of the palpable evidence. The Letter to the Hebrews, at the back of the Book, tells us:

> No discipline seems pleasant at the time, but painful. Later on, however, it produces a harvest of righteousness and peace for those who have been trained by it.[6]

The Letter of James carries the thought further.

> Consider it pure joy, my brothers, whenever you face trials of many kinds, because you know that the testing of your faith develops perseverance. Perseverance must finish its work so that you may be mature and complete, not lacking anything. . . . Blessed is the man who perseveres under trial, because when he has stood the test, he will receive the crown of life that God has promised to those who love him.[7]

Such words remind us of Francis Bacon's comparison of the Old Testament with the New:

> The virtue of prosperity is temperance, the virtue of adversity is fortitude, which in morals is the more heroic. Prosperity is the blessing of the Old Testament, adversity is the blessing of the New, which carries the greater benediction and the clearer revelation of God's favor.[8]

It may seem a bit "much" to leave us stranded on the beach and then ask us to call what we are going through "pure joy." But for the Christian the New Testament is clear: we endure hardness because it makes us better disciples of Jesus Christ. And as Bacon suggests, there are rewards in reconciling ourselves to this position. "Adversity is not without comforts and hopes." The New Testament spells it out: "Later on . . . righteousness and peace . . . and a crown of life."

Let's assume then for the moment that we move past the complaining stage and accept our situation as an opportunity for positive development and growth. After all, it was not God who spoke of rejection. Our feeling of rejection by God, like the Psalmist's, may be purely a subjective impression. There is no word from the fortress turning us away.

But that's just the trouble! There is no word from the fortress at all. If only it would speak! There it stands against the sky, so somber, so austere, so impenetrable—and so silent. Religion might be defined as man's recurring and perennial effort to make the fortress speak. Just for us to recognize it as being "there" is not enough; it provides no answer to the interrogations posed by human existence.

Perry Miller has characterized the seventeenth-century New England Puritans as a people who were "gifted—or cursed—with an overwhelming realization of an inexorable power at work not only in nature but in themselves, which they called God."[9] Such a description may not stand up historically, for it fails to make allowance for the Puritans' biblical base. But in any case it is wholly inadequate for us. To say that God is merely the Creator and we are his creatures is to open the door to a thousand questions. Why does he baffle us so? Why does he let us flounder out of one predicament into another, and each one worse? Why does he allow—oh, we can't begin to list the things that are wrong with the universe, from death and demons to hangnails.

We are back on the beach, trying to muster some faith and trust and hoping to make a virtue of our adversity. We're sure something is up there in that fortress, but what? Meanwhile, conditions on the beach are deteriorating. Waves are washing around our feet, and darkness has fallen. Something will have to be done and soon. In our desperation we send up a prayer.

THE CLEFT IN THE ROCK

We notice a light flickering in the distance. Apparently someone is coming along the beach. It is a small light, a torch, and it's moving toward us. But now our attention is distracted, because we hear at last a voice speaking to us from above; whether it is from the fortress we cannot tell. Because of the wind's velocity we catch only a phrase or two of what seems to be verses from the Bible: "I am who I am. . . . I the Lord do not change. . . . As you have done, it will be done to you. . . . Where were you when I laid the earth's foundation? . . ."[10]

The wind gives a final burst and dies away, and soon we hear a song echoing on the cliffs, a strange song with an oriental tune, almost a lament.

> He was despised and rejected by men,
>   a man of sorrows, and familiar with suffering.
> Like one from whom men hide their faces
>   he was despised, and we esteemed him not.
>
> Surely he took up our infirmities
>   and carried our sorrows,
> yet we considered him stricken by God,
>   smitten by him, and afflicted.
> But he was pierced for our transgressions,
>   he was crushed for our iniquities;
> the punishment that brought us peace was upon him,
>   and by his wounds we are healed.
> We all, like sheep, have gone astray,
>   each of us has turned to his own way;
> and the Lord has laid on him
>   the iniquity of us all.[11]

By this time the light has approached near to us, and we can vaguely make out a figure walking. We see it is a man clothed in a homespun robe. He is bearded and barefoot and has a familiar look. As he comes up to us, he greets us. A warm feeling spreads through our bodies; we feel as if we are old friends, as if we have known him since childhood. We want to stay near him, to feel the touch of his hand, even to hug him. All the frenetic anxiety over our dilemma has vanished. We don't mind a thing, not even that big high rock.

But it is toward the rock that he beckons us, to the base of the steep cliff. As we draw near it seems to us more forbidding than ever. The beach itself is strewn with various kinds of litter. By the light of our friend's torch, we thread our way between broken statuary and splintered ladders and other instruments people have used to try to shinny their way to God. We even recognize some of our own excess baggage that we once used as props to get closer to heaven—check stubs and resumés and bootstraps of varied shapes.

Now we are at the foot of the mighty fortress. So complete is the darkness we cannot see it, but we can feel the smooth wall with our hands. Our guide is flashing his light about, and we are astonished to see that he has located a cleft in the rock. He looks at us, then turns and leads the way inside.

As we follow him it occurs to us that we may never know the full mystery of the fortress; its silences, its recesses lie beyond us. But we don't need to, for into the obscure shadows has come a man with a light. He is one of us, and yet he obviously knows what we do not know. For he has taken us out of our grim circumstance into the shelter of the fortress —and we are delivered!

This is the best friend our stiff-necked and perverse human race has ever had. He is the Son of God, the Paraclete (1 John 2:1) who comes alongside us and stands up for us and pleads our cause—which is what the Psalmist asked for—and takes our place and bears our iniquity and delivers us from death and hell and saves our souls forever.

Do you believe that? Let me put it this way: Would you rather be trapped on that shallow beach, with the tide coming in and no escape route and the darkness falling? Or would you rather find a cleft in the rock and be rescued?

Nothing has really changed since the Psalmist asked, in Psalm 2:

> Why do the nations rage
> and the peoples plot in vain?[12]

Insecurity is the mood of the West. Turbulence is increasing in the Third World except where the iron heel crushes it. The suggestion has been made that we should have made a parking lot out of North Vietnam. Aside from humanitarian considerations, such a military move would not have kept the Cubans out of Africa or stopped the coup in Afghanistan. The arms race is escalating everywhere. Terrorism has become a political tool. Reactors are leaking. Armies are marching. As Pitirim Sorokin, the Harvard sociologist, expressed it, "All the Horses of the Apocalypse are rampaging on the planet as never before." And he adds, "Without the Kingdom of God we are doomed to a weary and torturing pilgrimage from calamity to calamity, from crisis to crisis."[13]

Would you like to get off this miserable beach? Would you like to find a place of refuge, a shelter from the forces of wickedness? Then follow Jesus into the cleft in the rock. That's where I went, and do you know what I found? (This is unbelievable.) A warm, well-lighted lobby, carpeted flooring and an express elevator waiting to take us to the top.

But now I was alone, for Jesus had gone back to the beach. The gate closed and the elevator began to move. Remembering how that fortress looked from the beach, I found my anxiety returning. Then music—beautiful choir music—filled the lift, and I heard a young voice singing:

> In my Father's house
> I shall dwell forever;
> In my Father's house
> there's plenty of room.

And I was at peace.

Send forth your light and your truth,
  let them guide me;
let them bring me to your holy mountain,
  to the place where you dwell.
          —Psalm 43:3

CHAPTER TWELVE

The Angel of Light

WHAT KIND OF LIGHT?

Out of our tears and suffering, out of the brutal pounding of the waves, out of the misery inflicted by cruel people and circumstances, we come at last to our real petition. We know now that escape is not enough. What good is it to be delivered from one dark corner to another, from one frustrating situation to perhaps a worse one?

We need light. Our thirst for God, translated, means we

want to *see* him, or at least some clear evidence of him; some trail he has marked for us or for someone else.

Most of us recall a time when we ached to see a loved one, ached with a longing so deep is seemed it could not be borne. Life without our beloved seemed so drab, so pointless—and so interminable. To thirst for God means feeling exactly that way. It's how God designed us: he wants us to feel that way about him. Our yearning for the One who made us is a continuing desire and quest for something we can never fully find here below. Not fully. But we can find enough!

The apostle Paul told the Athenians on Mars Hill that God created the race of human beings precisely "so that men would seek him and perhaps reach out for him and find him."[1] That word "reach out," from the Greek *psao*, to touch, is the word Homer used to describe the blinded giant Cyclops groping for his assailant, Ulysses. So we feel and grope for God, but we need light. We pray, Lord, send the light!

But what is light? Is the Psalmist talking about the physical properties of light? Hardly. He knows our need is not for increased wattage; we can't even stand the light we have. To look at the sun is to destroy our sight. Then does he mean intellectual light? We should know by now that the light of knowledge will not satisfy our thirst for God. Such information as our century has amassed is impressive, but it has not shown us the way out of our sins. Much of it is undigested, yet we keep feeding more into the computers daily, until it seems that the more we learn the less we know.

For two hundred years we have enjoyed the heritage of the so-called Age of Enlightenment. Many thought the race was gradually improving, but World War I torpedoed that opinion. Now the whole world knows what Bible Christians have always known: everything that human intelligence puts together is corruptible. Our minds are brilliant but tainted. We progress and regress at the same time. We pass laws and violate them as soon as they are on the books. We invent movable type and publish pornography. We wheel cars off the assembly line and into a freeway pileup. We invent telephones and make obscene calls. We parole the guilty and rip off the innocent. We launch satellites and spy on each other. We release the power of the atom and now all life is in jeopardy. Clearly it will take more than the light of intelligence to burn off the clouds of our iniquity.

In commenting on this passage—"Send forth your light and your truth"—Delitzsch brings out the moral element in the Psalmist's prayer. "Light and truth," he says, "are equivalent to mercy and truth. What is intended is the *light* of mercy or loving-kindness which is coupled with the *truth* of fidelity to the promises. . . . The light is that by which the will or purpose of love, which is God's most especial nature, becomes outwardly manifest."[2]

Delitzsch compares Psalm 43:3 with Psalm 57:3 which declares, "God sends his love and his faithfulness." He finds a similar thought in the "Song of Moses":

> "In your unfailing *love* you will lead
> the people you have redeemed.
> In your strength you will guide them
> to your holy dwelling."[3]

Alexander Maclaren adopts a similar interpretation, saying, "*Loving-kindness* and *faithfulness in fulfilling promises* [i.e., light and truth] are like two angels, dispatched from the presence chamber of God, to guide the exile's steps."[4] And according to J. A. Alexander, *light* in this passage represents "the favorable aspect of God."[5]

Now let us see what the New Testament says about light. In the first chapter of the First Letter of John we read, "God is light; in him there is no darkness at all." That is, the divine character cannot be portrayed in chiaroscuro; light and shade go well in Rembrandt, not in deity. We read further and come upon a fresh interpretation: "Anyone who claims to be in the light but hates his brother is still in the darkness. Whoever loves his brother lives in the light, and there is nothing in him to make him stumble. But whoever hates his brother is in the darkness and walks around in the darkness; he does not know where he is going, because the darkness has blinded him."[6]

Here we have a theology of the New Testament. Love is light and hate is darkness. When we ask God to send forth his

light, as the Psalmist did, it is because he *is* light. But by light
we are to understand not just the light of the sun, or the light
of learning, or some edifying light such as the light of a noble
idea. John is talking about the light of love and specifically
about the way we treat each other. Not the way we treat God,
but the way we treat each other.

Do you hear that, John Milton? You wrote about education
but neglected to educate your daughters. Do you hear it,
Sherwood Wirt? You preach sermons on love, but show impa-
tience and irritation around the house and criticize other
Christians.

If John's interpretation of "light" as "love" is to hold up, it
needs to be validated by other Scriptures. What do we find?
In his same First Letter appear the words, "If we walk in the
light, as he is in the light, we have fellowship with one
another."[7] And in the Gospel of John, by the same author,
we find a similar exposition: "Light [that is, Jesus Christ] has
come into the world, but men loved darkness instead of light
because their deeds were evil. Everyone who does evil hates
the light, . . . but whoever lives by the truth comes into the
light."[8]

The beginning of Isaiah 61 is a well-known passage that
Jesus quoted in the synagogue at Nazareth. It speaks of actions which can only be construed as deeds of love: opening
eyes that are blind, freeing captives from prison, releasing
from the dungeon those who sit in darkness. The passage is
preceded by the prophetic and messianic statement, "I
will . . . make you a light for the Gentiles."[9]

As a final example, in Romans the apostle Paul sums up the
Ten Commandments under "this one rule: 'Love your neighbor as yourself,'" adding that such love "is the fulfillment of
the law." Then he moves easily to the imagery of light: "The
night is nearly over; the day is almost here. So let us put aside
the deeds of darkness and put on the armor of light."[10]

LIGHT AS LOVE

Now I have an exercise to propose to you. Take a concor-
dance and look up the word "light." Mark the references to

"light" in the Bible and then check them out. Wherever you find the word "light," *and it seems appropriate*, render it by the word "love." If you are reluctant to do it, fearing that such a proposal unwarrantably alters the sacred text, let me point out that it is just an exercise. It is intended to bring out shades of meaning that will be instructive and helpful. When you have finished the exercise, throw it away and go back to the traditional wording.

To illustrate, I will take a sampling from the Old and New Testaments. First, Genesis 1:2:

> . . . The Spirit of God was hovering over the waters. And God said, "Let there be love," and there was love.

Then Psalm 36:9:

> For with you is the fountain of life; in your love we see love.

And Isaiah 9:2:

> The people walking in darkness have seen a great love.

And Matthew 5:16:

> "Let your love shine before men, that they may see your good deeds and praise your Father in heaven."

And John 1:9:

> The true love that gives love to every man was coming into the world.

If we follow the interpretation of First John and equate darkness with hate, an even more vivid rendition results in John 12:46:

> "I have come into the world as love, so that no one who believes in me should stay in the darkness of hate."

And in Romans 13:12:

> Put aside the deeds of hate and put on the armor of love.

Holiness, for many of us, is a carrot on a stick. If we have to love everybody regardless of their odd looks and strange speech, we had better give up. We'll never make it to the mountain of the Lord. At least that's the way we feel; we consider ourselves spiritually, physically, and psychologically unable to love certain people. We're like the man who said to A. B. Simpson, founder of the Christian and Missionary Alliance, "I do not want to love some people; I should not respect myself if I did; I take a real pleasure in disliking them."[11]

To make love the rationale of the universe, therefore, is to unfit us to live in it. Our own natures have thwarted us and we are undone. We may still go to church, but as far as our thirst for God goes, we'll try to forget about it.

Such was my condition in the winter of 1971–72, when I paid a visit to the Canadian Revival in Winnipeg, Manitoba. If the people there had urged me to "repent," I would have been off the hook. Repent? Naturally I had repented. I went that route years ago; how else do you think I became a Christian?

> Gone, gone, gone, gone
> All my sins are gone.
> Now my soul is free
> And in my heart's a song.

Of course they weren't gone, and furthermore, in my heart there wasn't a song. But let the record show that I had repented.

What the Canadians did say to me was, "You have to face up to your problem. You have to deal with it." They didn't even know I had a problem, though they guessed as much. But it was right in this vicinity that I was having trouble. I couldn't love some people, didn't see any reason to love, had no inclination to love, wasn't about to repent because I didn't love, and had plenty of justification for my position, which I was prepared to defend before any church court.

In other places I have related what happened to me in Canada.[12] Briefly, I returned to my editor's chair in Minneapolis, and at the behest of some local pastors, invited a husband-and-wife team to come from Winnipeg to the Twin Cities for a weekend. They spoke in four churches and held an

"Afterglow"—a late-night prayer meeting in which people asked for prayer for themselves. On the night of January 9, 1972, I prayed and asked to be filled with the Holy Spirit. Later in the week I sensed that in some way God had touched my life with a fresh infusion of love.

It was following that experience that I discovered the fourth chapter of First John—or rediscovered it. And being now filled with the Spirit of God and with love, I grappled the words of that chapter to my heart:

> Dear friends, let us love one another, for love comes from God. Everyone who loves has been born of God and knows God. Whoever does not love does not know God, because God is love. . . . No one has ever seen God; but if we love each other, God lives in us and his love is made complete in us. We know that we live in him and he in us, because he has given us of his Spirit. . . . If anyone says, "I love God," yet hates his brother, he is a liar. For anyone who does not love his brother, whom he has seen, cannot love God, whom he has not seen.[13]

Cameron Townsend, founder of the Wycliffe Bible Translators, tells of reading that passage to a bedridden Soviet official in Russia and seeing the man reduced to tears.

In my book *Afterglow* I commented on a passage in Revelation 2 in which the risen Jesus tells the writer, John, to inform the church at Ephesus that he has something against it, namely, that the church has left its first love. I suggested that the "first love" might have been the Christians' love for each other, since that was a major theme of the New Testament writers.[14]

Since studying the rest of the passage, I have noted that Jesus warned the Ephesian Christians that if they did not change their ways, he would "remove your lampstand" out of its place. The lampstand gave light. What Jesus was apparently saying in verse five of Revelation 2 was, no love, no light.

DRYWELL AND WEAKREED

After I had drafted the previous few pages I read them to some fellow-writers who posed serious questions to me:

"What is your definition of love? Is there a difference between love for one's family and Christian love? Or a difference between liking a person and loving that person as a Christian? How do you deal with someone who is being obnoxious? And how does the Holy Spirit give us the love that we can't seem to find in ourselves for certain people—or peoples?"

Faced with these challenges, I found myself praying with the Psalmist, "Lord, send the light!" Let me approach the questions candidly but indirectly.

Imagine a person named Sampson Drywell whom you might have known in different capacities. First, Sampson was your business partner, but he withdrew all the funds from your joint bank account and skipped town. You haven't seen or heard from him since.

Or, Sampson was a licensed contractor who built a house for you, but did such poor work that you were forced to spend thousands of dollars in repairs and reconstruction. You filed suit, charging incompetence, and the case is now in the courts.

Or, Sampson was an obstetrician who bungled the delivery of your child. Today you cannot look at the child without being reminded of the attending physician's inexcusable carelessness.

Now let us change the gender and imagine a person named Lorina Weakreed. She was your babysitter. One day while she was watching television, your child slipped into the kitchen, found a bottle in the cupboard under the sink, and swallowed a poisonous substance. When Lorina discovered what had happened, she failed to notify a doctor who might have saved the child's life.

Or, Lorina destroyed the morale of your office staff by spreading rumors about your behavior that were untrue.

Or, Lorina made love to your husband and broke up your marriage. She is now living with your husband in a nearby apartment, and you have been informed that he is bragging about having the time of his life—and is attending church.

These illustrations are enough, I think, to dispel any illusions one might have that once we become Christians, it will be easy to love everyone. Actually, when one considers the whole spectrum of human wickedness, they are rather mild examples.

To show that he made no distinction between family love and Christian love, Jesus asked, "Who are my mother and my brothers?" And he added, "Whoever does God's will is my brother and sister and mother."[15] He expanded the point in the parable of the Good Samaritan, which identifies one's neighbor as the person in need, regardless of race or creed.[16]

Most of the New Testament was not written to people who were spiritually dead in their sins; it was addressed to people who were already Christians. The New Testament was written to get believers to love each other. Jesus again and again reminded his disciples that their first duty was not to evangelize but to demonstrate love for each other. I do not intend to try to define that love, any more than I would define what it means to be born anew. But I will say that it was love with both a vertical and horizontal direction: "We love because he first loved us."[17] And it was a love that expressed itself in practical gestures and actions.

Jesus did not distinguish between liking and loving a person. We don't know, for example, whether the Samaritan in his parable "liked" the victim of mugging on the Jericho road, but the Samaritan certainly demonstrated love toward him. "Liking" seems to depend to an extent on similarity of tastes and natural affinities, as well as characteristics and qualities that one esteems in another. But to say that one can love a person without liking him is risky, for it implies that a person with a cold and unaffectionate attitude is really showing love. The semantic difficulties are obvious; yet unless Christian love is poured out by the Holy Spirit—demonstrably—it may well do more harm than good.

How can we *like*—let alone *love* such people as Sampson Drywell and Lorina Weakreed? We are forced back to the Psalmist's prayer, "Lord, send forth your light," not just to illuminate our minds but to fill up what is lacking in our hearts.

The meaning of the Cross "came into sync" for me only when my heart understood what my head had long known: that Calvary was the end of the road, not just for my Savior, but for me also. He shed his blood there for the sin of the world and my sin, after which God raised him from the tomb, after which our risen Lord sent the Paraclete, the Holy Spirit, into the church at Pentecost.

If I am to participate in what happened at Pentecost, as I now understand the New Testament, I must first participate in Calvary. If I am to be filled with the Spirit and receive a supernatural impartation of the love of God, I must first be emptied of self, must be crucified with Christ. While this crucifixion actually took place two thousand years ago under the jurisdiction of Pontius Pilate, it needs to be appropriated by faith.

Once this happens to a person, he simply dies to self. He moves off the premises and leaves the rest to God. I have stopped worrying about my self-image, because now my self is lost in serving and helping others.

I've learned that it's not necessary to track down Sampson Drywell or Lorina Weakreed and say to them, "Something marvelous has happened to me. I used to consider you obnoxious, but now I just love you." We can let the Spirit do all that through us. His timing is better than ours. He prearranges the communications and supplies the love as needed—again, through us. He has an abundant supply; no need to be anxious on that score. But before his ministry can take over a life, there has to be an emptying in which bitterness is neutralized, hostility dissolved, resentment canceled out.

Don't expect it to be all strawberry shortcake. It wasn't for me, and it won't be for you. Death is seldom easy, and dying to self is a kind of death. I found tension as I sought the leading of the Spirit in this new life of love. But it was a creative tension that produced some beautiful things, and as time passed it became easier to say, "The Lord has done this, and it is marvelous in our eyes."[18]

It has occurred to me, and to others I'm sure, that when our

Lord was in the Garden of Gethsemane he might have recalled the Psalmist's words: "Send forth your light and your truth, let them guide me; let them bring me to your holy mountain." If he did pray those words, then perhaps Jesus followed them with his, "Yet not as I will, but as you will."[19]

And what Maclaren calls "the two angels," light and truth, then guided our Savior to the holy mountain where he laid down his life in obedience to his Father—for us. And he left behind a message of two words: "Follow me."

CHAPTER THIRTEEN

The Angel of Truth

Send forth your light and your truth,
  let them guide me;
let them bring me to your holy mountain,
  to the place where you dwell.
            —Psalm 43:3

THE BIBLE AS TRUTH

A prominent resident of the Middle East has been banished from his country for political reasons. He is aware that back home he may be marked for assassination, yet he yearns to return. Each day, according to custom, he faithfully prays to God. He asks God to end his exile and lead him back where he belongs.

This man is not a Christian. What kind of prayer do you think he would offer? Would he go the violent route and ask that his enemies be eliminated by a natural disaster or a plague or a revolution? Perhaps he would ask for a series of heart attacks or poisonings. Or perhaps he would pray God to send a legion of angels with drawn swords to discomfit the foe. What do you think?

The Middle East resident I have in mind is the person who wrote this Psalm. It is noteworthy that he prayed for none of the things I have mentioned; instead he asked God to send light and truth to guide him. Wouldn't you agree that we could learn from such a person?

He prayed for truth. Was he thinking of New Testament truth? There was no New Testament; and it is unlikely that he had access in exile to such portions of the Old Testament as then existed. But he composed this prayer, which became part of the Old Testament.

And a beautiful prayer it is. I repeat it aloud, and the freshness and uniqueness of God's Word sweeps over me. I note that even though the Psalmist is praying out of personal anguish, he is not bitter; even though he feels utterly forsaken, he continues to call upon his God. A dozen immediate personal needs may be clamoring for attention; a hundred circumstances may seem to him to demand instant change; yet he limits his appeal to God to a request for light and truth.

Joseph Stalin once asserted that there is no such thing as eternal truth. Now Stalin is an unhappy memory we would sooner forget, while the truth lives on. That's the way it is with God's Word; the forge wears out the hammers.

As students of our environment we can break new ground in the science of human behavior; we can assess the results of botany, astrophysics, ecology, and a thousand other branches of knowledge; we can develop theories and hypotheses and erect philosophical systems on the basis of defined principles. But when it comes to truth—revealed truth—we have nowhere else to turn but to the Old and New Testaments.

What these documents disclose is not only truth about human beings (which can be corroborated in the Koran or the Bhagavad-Gita or the *Wall Street Journal* or the sheriff's report), but truth about God. And this disclosure is unique.

Let me illustrate. A century ago the New England Quaker poet, John Greenleaf Whittier, wrote,

> Yet, in the maddening maze of things,
>   And tossed by storm and flood,
> To one fixed trust my spirit clings:
>   I know that God is good![1]

For curiosity's sake, I would like to know where the poet got his information. How does he know that God is good? How does he know anything about God's character?

When we search for the answer in human literature we blunder into a swarm of contradictory statements about the nature of God and encounter such concepts as substance and essence and reality. We cross into the kingdom of myth and saga. We even find an extraordinary number of persons themselves claiming to be God. At the end of our search we despair of discovering truth and call it unattainable or nonexistent.

Facts we can handle. Facts speak for themselves. But truth—the understanding of the meaning of things, of the true situation—is beyond us. Then we turn to a strange, ancient book, composed at odd times over many centuries in a remote corner of the world by a people who claimed (as many others have claimed) to be in touch with God. We pick up this book. We say of it, "This is God's Word. This is truth."

At that moment we are no longer lost, consigned to a frail raft, adrift on the sea of relativism with no land in sight. We have reached a rock of safety.

Many people prefer the unsteady raft because, they tell us, "That's the way things are. There's nothing certain but uncertainty." If they are pointed to Scripture, they reject it because to them it is any one of the following:

A crashing bore.

A collection of inconsistencies.

An elongated sermon containing moral maxims they have no desire to live up to.

A useless artifact.

A mine of misinformation on Mediterranean cultures.

A literary document rather less interesting than others from the past, such as *The Iliad*.

A means of livelihood for obscure scholars.

A charm or amulet used by mediums and others to inculcate magical powers.

A source book for charlatans, cozeners, flim-flammers and con artists.

To turn from such sophisticated value judgments and approach the Bible as *truth* is to enter a new world. It is to uncover the skeins of Western culture and civilization. More than that, it is to learn that God still sends forth truth out of his Word to guide those who ask for it.

JESUS AND SCRIPTURE

"Our claim," says John R. W. Stott, the English writer, "is that God has revealed Himself by speaking; that this divine (or God-breathed) speech has been written down and preserved in Scripture; and that Scripture is, in fact, God's word written, which therefore is true and reliable and has divine authority over men."[2]

On what does he base such an audacious claim? On the teaching of the church? On the assumptions of the various authors of the Bible? On the Bible's prestige and world-wide influence? Stott says No. "The first and foremost reason why Christians believe in the divine inspiration and authority of Scripture is . . . because of what Jesus Christ Himself said. Since He endorsed the authority of Scripture, we are bound to conclude that His authority and Scripture's authority stand or fall together. . . . We bow to the authority of Scripture because we bow to the authority of Christ. . . .

"All the available evidence confirms that Jesus Christ reverently assented in His mind and submitted in His life to the authority of the Old Testament. He also seems to have foreseen the need for Scriptures of the New Testament corresponding to the Scriptures of the Old. He made provision for the New Testament by authorizing His apostles to teach in His name. The apostles were to be His personal representatives, endowed with His authority. . . . He said that the Holy Spirit would lead them into all truth, would bring to their remembrance what He had spoken to them, and would show them things to come."[3]

So we find that when Jesus said, "I am the truth," he regrouped the world. Instead of conceding any number of existing attitudes people might take toward the Bible, he reduced that number to two: those who believe him and those who don't. Reason requires us to conclude that if we believe Jesus is truth, we can only believe that his position on Scripture is truth.

The supportive position Jesus took with regard to the divine origin of the Old and New Testaments should be enough to convince any follower of his. Unfortunately the issue is not so simple. A vigorous debate has erupted in recent years, not over questions of authority or revelation or verbal inspiration, but over the Bible's *inerrancy*. The controversy has proved bewildering and embarrassing to many Christians who have friends holding opposing views.

I do not like the term "inerrancy," yet I find myself in a dilemma whenever I get away from it. The truth is that if the Bible is not trustworthy, then Jesus is not trustworthy, and the Spirit of God is not trustworthy. And if that be the case, where is the love of God which the Spirit is so eager to pour into our hearts, according to Romans 5:5? Where is the supernatural power declared to be available to us? Where is the weapon which, when we grasp it, will turn back the Evil One? Jesus said to Satan, "It is written." What if we can't say that? What if all we can say is, "Once it was written in a specific cultural context and addressed to a particular situation that no longer exists"?

The highly respectable theological seminary in which I enrolled a year before Pearl Harbor was known for its radically critical approach to scholarship. Unfortunately what respect I had for the Bible was dissipated soon after I entered in a fog of redactors and pseudo-authors. It was customary at this school to teach that the date of the authorship of the Book of Daniel was extremely late; that the historicity of John's Gospel was suspect; and that Paul had a clever imitator who ghosted Ephesians and the Pastoral Epistles.

Not being a committed Christian at the time, I saw no reason to challenge the trendy teaching, but one of my fellow-students from a conservative denomination did. When asked to conduct a chapel service, he created a stir among the faculty by announcing from the pulpit, "The road to hell is paved with the skulls of scholars."

Today certain evangelical authorities are teaching in evangelical seminaries that the date of Daniel is late and that Paul did not write Ephesians. The wheel has come full circle. I could wish that my student friend were around to deliver his message a few more times. The fact is that for every liberal position taken upon the Scriptures, there is a conservative position, equally cogent and equally well supported by textual and linguistic evidence, as well as by the expert opinions of both Jewish and Christian scholars.

During my sixteen years as editor of *Decision* magazine I wrote more editorials about the authority of the Bible than any other subject. One reason was that I knew a lot of my readers were struggling with the question. Another was that I had long struggled with it. Not until I had been an ordained minister for eleven years did the Lord give me peace about my relationship to his Word. I then ceased to be a non-Bible person and joined the Bible people. I stopped pretending to be an authority on Scripture and recognized that Scripture was an authority on me.

Martin Luther called the canonical books of the Old and New Testaments a golden ring that cannot be broken. They are to be received wholly as God's Word and not merely in part. They cannot speak truth in one place and falsehood in another. If we are looking to the Holy Spirit to renew the church, why not begin here? Let's teach in season and out that the Scriptures are the divinely inspired Word by which the Spirit of God witnesses to men and women the saving truth of Jesus Christ. Let's declare the plenary inspiration of the Bible, as Theodore Mueller says, "in the full sense of the word," recognizing that the written Word of Scripture is always indissolubly joined with the power of the Holy Spirit. [4]

STEADY AS SHE GOES

In 1938 I served briefly on a single voyage as quartermaster aboard an eighty-foot patrol boat of the Alaska Game Commission, the M. S. *Teal*. We sailed for the better part of a week in rough weather from Valdez to Juneau across the Gulf of Alaska, on a course east three quarters north. When we arrived at the foot of Gastineau Channel between Douglas Island and the mainland, I was at the wheel. Captain Cole, the skipper, then took over and altered our course to head us northward toward Juneau. He pointed to the new compass reading and said, "Steady as she goes." I took the wheel again.

The day was bright, and as we cruised along, I estimated that we were well out in midchannel, but noticed that we seemed to be edging toward the banks on the mainland. I eased off a couple of points and steered the *Teal* straight up channel. In a few minutes Captain Cole came on the bridge and checked our bearings. He snapped, "You're off course! Go back to the reading I gave you." My dead reckoning had led me to believe one thing, but the chart indicated something else. We were not in midchannel. Following my intuition might have led to shipwreck.

God has given us a chart and has marked on it the shoals and hidden currents of life, as well as the clear channels. That chart represents the truth. We can deviate from it and even draw up our own chart, but the result could well be disaster.

As it happens, we don't need to know where all the threats to navigation are; all we need to know is where the deep channel lies. Bernie May of Jungle Aviation and Radio Service (JAARS) tells of flying in the Peruvian Andes as a young missionary pilot and being asked to take three American businessmen to a remote village. The men came out to the airstrip where the tiny plane stood and they gazed at the mountains dubiously. One man asked, "Captain, are you sure you know where all the mountain ridges and peaks are between here and Tingo Maria?"

Bernie replied, "No, sir, but I know where they're not. And that's the course we're going to fly."[5]

The Bible is our blueprint, our chart to get through life and arrive safely at our final destination. We ignore it at our peril, not because it is the best we can come up with, but because it didn't come from us; it came from God. It carries the stamp of divine authority and has earned its right to speak. It knows the route.

In 1963 the *Mona Lisa* was being exhibited in the United States. As the crowds filed past the painting, occasional derogatory comments were heard: "What's so wonderful about that?" But the *Mona Lisa* was not on trial.

A commercial layout artist in the Middle East once criticized to me the Renaissance master painters, saying that many of their works were poorly executed. But Leonardo and Raphael and Michelangelo are not on trial today. It is we who are on trial as we evaluate their works.

In the same way the Bible has stood the test of time and is not on trial. We are on trial as we sit under its teachings. When we denigrate God's Word, we reveal something not so much about the Bible as about ourselves. As a child of God I have the freedom and even the right to expound the Bible, assuming anyone will listen. But I do not have the right as a child of God to impugn its truth. If I exercise a right I do not have, I lose the right I do have.

Today there seems to be good will in many quarters toward what is called civil religion or religion-in-general. Government prayer breakfasts are popular; Bible sales are impressive. But in the marketplace where the world does its business, the authority of God's Word is weak. Marjoes, charlatans, and imposters have lowered the Bible's reputation, while other and more ominous doctrines are put into play. W. B. Yeats, in his poem "The Second Coming," describes the scene.

> The falcon cannot hear the falconer;
> Things fall apart; the centre cannot hold;
> Mere anarchy is loosed upon the world,
> The blood-dimmed tide is loosed, and everywhere
> The ceremony of innocence is drowned;
> The best lack all conviction, while the worst
> Are full of passionate intensity.[6]

The crisis of authority in modern life, according to Dr. Klaas Runia, is the result of our effort to create a secular society, which is by definition a society without the authority of God.

We human beings are so constituted that we need an inner gyroscope to give us moral balance and control. God's Word meets that purpose. When we reject it, we take the consequences. Kirilov put it brassily in Dostoevsky's novel *The Possessed:* "If God is dead, everything is permissible. If God does not exist, then I am God."

The result of the loss of authority is evident everywhere today, even on bumper stickers which say QUESTION AUTHORITY. Change is having a loosening effect. To speak biblically, it would seem that the restrainer is no longer restraining, and the adversary's hand is reaching for the human throat. In such circumstances who can do anything? Who can prevent this careening juggernaut of a society from ridding itself of itself?

Now perhaps we can begin to fathom the depths of the Forty-second and Forty-third Psalms. We can begin to pray, "Send forth your light and your truth, let them guide us."

Our Century of Progress was born at a time where there seemed only one way to go: forward. As it draws to a close we find it necessary to change direction and go back. We must become not more exciting, but more prudent. Not neater, but wiser. Back to the rock whence we were hewn, to the venerable, ancestral, time-honored principles from which our social order sprang. Back to Scripture.

We have gone forward too fast, and for our sakes and our children's we need to go back to the solid verities embedded in all human societies—and especially to the clear truths enshrined in God's Word.

But when we do, let's go carefully. In a universe filled with mystery let's not claim too much. Robert Ferm says that some of the people who boast of their belief in the Scriptures most loudly do so because secretly they have gnawing doubts.[7] Let's not join them.

Let's not go about asserting that the Bible has "all the answers." That is cheap talk. If the Bible has all the answers, why is the Psalmist (who authored part of the Bible) crying out so desperately, asking God to send light and truth?

What the Bible gives are the answers we need. Its precepts are a lamp to our feet and a light to our path. Our acknowledgement of scriptural authority should be like a man who falls off the deck of an ocean liner and accepts the authority of a lifebuoy thrown to him. As far as he is concerned, it's there, it's dependable, it does the job. Just so by guiding and protecting us, the Bible shows us how to live in the human family. It teaches us how we can be set free from the bondage of sin and filled with the Holy Spirit and with love. It teaches us how to overcome disappointment and how to meet adversity, sickness, and death.

That will do for a start.

CHAPTER FOURTEEN

The Mountain

Send forth your light and your truth,
  let them guide me;
let them bring me to your holy mountain,
  to the place where you dwell.
          —Psalm 43:3

THE HOUSE OF GOD

More than one critical commentator of these verses insists that the Psalmist was not thirsting for God so much as he was homesick for Jerusalem. His yearning for the "holy mountain" is construed as a desire to get back to where the action was. So the scene might be compared to Athanasius in exile, Napoleon on St. Helena, or the Ayatollah Khomeini in Paris waiting for a plane to Teheran. The Psalmist was a V.I.P. in the temple of Mount Zion, according to this interpretation, and the god he was importuning was a kind of tribal deity or domestic spook who inhabited the precincts. Composing the Forty-second and Forty-third Psalms represented his attempt to get some kind of supernatural pizzazz going.

If I believed that, I would feed these pages to a shredding machine. But perhaps the Hebrews were not as totem-minded and tribalistic as a few oriental scholars would have us believe. Perhaps they did not keep their God in a box, but worshiped him as Jesus did, in spirit and in truth. The best way to settle the question is to consult Scripture. First, Deuteronomy 32:6:

> Is he not your Father, your Creator,
>   who made you and formed you?

Then the following lines from Psalm 50:

> "I have no need of a bull from your stall
>   or of goats from your pens,
> for every animal of the forest is mine,
>   and the cattle on a thousand hills.
> I know every bird in the mountains,
>   and the creatures of the field are mine.
> If I were hungry I would not tell you,
>   for the world is mine, and all that is in it."[1]

Then let us listen to the prayer that King Solomon offered at the dedication of the first temple, as recorded in 1 Kings 8:

> "O Lord, God of Israel, there is no God like you in heaven above or on earth below. . . . But will God really dwell on earth? The heavens, even the highest heaven, cannot contain you. How much less this temple I have built! . . . Hear the cry and the prayer that your servant is praying in your presence this day. May your eyes be open toward this temple night and day, this place of which you said, 'My Name shall be there,' so that you will hear the prayer . . . of your servant and of your people Israel when they pray toward this place. Hear from heaven, your dwelling place, and when you hear, forgive."[2]

And finally the famed passage in Isaiah 66 that was quoted by the martyr Stephen:

This is what the Lord says:
"Heaven is my throne
and the earth is my footstool.
Where is the house you will build for me?
Where will my resting place be?
Has not my hand made all these things,
and so they came into being?"[3]

Such passages bring out what most Jewish and Christian scholars readily accept, that for the Psalmist, Mount Zion was not a place where God "lived" in any local sense. The holy mountain was a place of prayer, a sacred site, where the worshiper could lift up his hands and glorify the God of heaven. To speak of the temple site as the "place where God dwells" would be like the deacon of a local church referring to his church building as "God's house." As Alexander Maclaren says, "The actual return to the temple is desired because thereby new praise will be occasioned. Not mere bodily presence there, but that joyful outpouring of triumph and gladness, is the object of the Psalmist's longing."[4]

The whole point of the Psalmist's asking for light and truth and guidance, then, is not to get to the holy mountain so much as to get to God for the purpose of worshiping him.[5] The best evidence that the Psalmist's thirst for God was genuine and not geographical may be found in the two key words of his prayer, "light and truth." Perhaps we can summarize what we have learned about these words.

Light. Light as radiance can blind us. Light as knowledge is corruptible. But light as love is the essence of God himself; it is precisely because God is love that the human race refuses to let go of him in spite of the pundits. Whether the universe is a meaningless configuration of atoms or whether it is neutral or even friendly no longer concerns many of us; we feel we have spent too much time already in such cul-de-sacs. We want to know if Lady Julian is right when she says that the universe is made for love. If she is, then I for one want to join Ethan the Ezrahite or whoever else wrote the Eighty-ninth Psalm:

With my mouth I will make your faithfulness known
    through all generations.
I will declare that your love stands firm forever,
    that you established your faithfulness in heaven itself.[6]

Truth. What the Forty-third Psalm tells us (and the Eighty-ninth Psalm underscores) is that truth is something a believer can depend on. It is a divine promise that will not fail, a conscious integrity in the heavenly Father on which one can stake his life. It is truth because it's true. God's fidelity stands fixed and firm forever. It is established in heaven and makes, as Robert Louis Stevenson said of grace, the nails and axles of the universe.[7]

Not only is truth embedded in the nature of things, but it is enshrined in writing. The Psalmist did not, we can imagine, realize he was writing Holy Scripture, but the Spirit of God did. The Psalmist asked God to send forth truth. His prayer was answered; we were given God's Word.

One other comment needs to be added, this one from an ancient source. The early rabbis, in a "midrash," declared that when the Psalmist prayed "Send forth thy light and thy truth," "thy light" was actually the prophet Elijah and "thy truth" was—"the Messiah, the son of David!"[8]

THE RISK OF WORSHIP

Worship is one of the most thrilling words in the human lexicon. To "worship the Lord in the beauty of holiness"[9] is to feel the heart lifted out of itself on to a different plane where all is purity and light. The core of the religious instinct is the experience of worship. It takes us back, not just to the temple and the tabernacle of the Hebrews, or to the sticks and idols of other tribes, but clear back to Eden where our ancestor walked with God in the cool of the day.

An enormous amount of humbug has been written about worship, much of it by religious-minded people who insist that we ought to do it the way *they* do it. Any other kind of worship, as they see it, is valid but not regular, or regular but not valid, or neither one. One person is said to have remarked to an acquaintance, "Of course it's quite true, we all do worship the same God—you in your way, and I in *his*."

Many churchgoers have at least a hazy idea as to what true worship is, though they may not be able to express it in words. They recognize it as one of the few weekly activities in which they engage that could be said to be unselfishly motivated. Actually what goes on in the human heart in the way of worship is a secret between the individual and God; it cannot be used to impress people. Other worshipers see merely the externals, which may or may not be sincere. Christian youth are currently singing an English chorus that reflects an authentic New Testament attitude of worship:

> Let's forget about ourselves
> and concentrate on him
> and worship him. . . .
> Worship Christ the Lord.[10]

But suppose you have to prepare a paper or a talk on the subject of Christian worship. You visit a library or a religious bookstore and look for the section headed "Worship." You'll find that everything but the Equal Rights Amendment and the Boy Scout Oath has been placed in this category. In the interest of clarity, therefore, let me narrow down the activities that can be properly called "worship" to something like the following:

Serving God
Praising God in song and spoken word
Repenting
Praying
Meditating on God's Word
Participating in the liturgy
Bringing an offering
Celebrating Holy Communion
Visiting the sick, the poor, and those in prison

Such activities appear to meet the biblical standards of worship when they are engaged in with reverence and sincerity.

If worship is one of the most exciting and exalting words in our language, it is also one of the most dangerous. In its name human beings have committed unbelievable atrocities against each other. Are you ready for this? Consider a Catholic pope reading his breviary while listening to the anguished cries of his cardinals tortured in an adjoining room at his command. Or an Anglican archbishop tracking down Puritan ministers, clapping them into filthy prisons, and fining them heavily for appearing in church without robes. Or the pious Protestant citizens of a New England state applying a three-corded whip twenty times to the back of a Quaker woman who preferred not to receive Communion when she went to church. Or black slaves being herded up the back steps of a Protestant church into "nigger heaven" to hear a white preacher harangue them from the Bible about servants obeying their masters.

But we should not be too critical of the past. In our own time the worship of God (unless it is done "our" way) is forbidden in many parts of the world. In North America the spread of cult and demon worship and the renewed popularity of the "black mass" should be enough to keep Christians humble.

In view of the wide divergence of opinion as to the proper way to render honor, glory, and praise to almighty God, we should look to the source of our faith for guidance.

THE GLOW

What can the New Testament tell us about worship? Can it really take us past the outer observances into the inner Presence of the living God? First let us look at the attitude Jesus took toward the worship of his Father in heaven.

1. Jesus regularly attended services in a synagogue on the Sabbath, but he was not always pleased by what went on there. Like the Hebrew prophets before him, he strongly emphasized the spiritual side of worship over the ritualistic and ceremonial.

2. He criticized the use of "vain repetitions" and the parading of piety by religious leaders in their public praying, indicating that his Father prefers secret prayer. Much of his own worship was private.

3. He attended ceremonial services at the temple in Jerusalem on several occasions, but he did not approve of the temple's commercial activities and expressed his indignation forcefully. He further predicted the temple's downfall and, presumably, the end of the sacrificial system.

4. He declared that worship of God should be "in spirit and in truth," and that it is real and acceptable only when it stems from, or leads to, worthy action.[11]

Within a generation after the Crucifixion, historical events brought tremendous changes in Israel's worship as the temple was destroyed and animal sacrifices ceased. In the days immediately following Pentecost, the disciples of Jesus would gather in the temple daily to teach and witness to the resurrection of Christ. After some confrontations with the authorities, the disciples discontinued the practice, and even before the leveling of the temple by the Romans in 70 A.D., Christians had begun to gather in houses for worship.

At such meetings no one in particular seems to have been the appointed leader. At times it was evidently a woman. Worship consisted of prayer, reading the Scriptures, singing, offerings, witnessing and sharing, the preaching of the Gospel, the "love feast" or *agape*, and the kiss of peace. The *agape* was the breaking of bread which has come down to us as the service of Holy Communion, instituted by Christ at the Last Supper and intended by him to be repeated by his followers in memory of his atoning sacrifice.

All these elements of worship except the kiss of peace are present in one form or another in today's church services. Furthermore, some churches still have the glow that characterized those early group meetings in Jerusalem, Antioch, Samaria, Philippi, and other places. But many churches have lost it and are wistfully wondering, Why? What has happened? Is it our Scriptures? (Perhaps the language is outmoded; we'll get some new Bibles.) Is it the singing? (Let's switch to another hymnbook.) Is it the preaching? ("We'll take action at the next meeting. . . .")

No, the problem is not at this end, but at the other. Worship is *worth-ship*. It has to do with God, his worthiness, his

majesty, his honor, his power, his love. It is the business of
giving God what is his due; of reverencing his holy name, and
adoring his attributes, and loving him for himself. When we
tinker with methods and modes of worship it may mean we
are ignoring the end we have in view. It's possible for us to
come to the holy mountain, the place where God dwells, and
forget even why we came!

The secret of worship, whether individual or collective, is
the presence of the Spirit of Truth. He takes our eyes off
people and things and fixes them on Jesus. He reminds us that
the secret of our Lord's ministry was not his arguments with
the Pharisees or his weekly attendance at synagogue. The
code to Jesus' ministry was the filling of the Holy Spirit. With
all his genius and spiritual insight, the Psalmist did not em-
phasize in this Psalm what is so beautifully brought out in
Psalm 139: *when we are filled with God, we are never off the
mountain.*

> Where can I go from your Spirit?
> Where can I flee from your presence?
> If I go up to the heavens, you are there;
> if I make my bed in the depths, you are there. . . .
> even the darkness will not be dark to you;
> the night will shine like the day. . . .[12]

In church or out, at prayers or not, it is all the same with the
Spirit. Brother Lawrence, the humble seventeenth-century
lay Carmelite monk, told the Abbé de Beaufort

> that for him the time of prayer was no different from any other
> time, that he retired to pray when Father Prior told him to do
> so, but that he neither desired nor asked for this since his most
> absorbing work did not divert him from God. . . . That he was
> very aware of his faults and was not dismayed by them, that he
> confessed them to God and did not ask him to excuse them;
> but that after doing so he returned in peace to his usual prac-
> tice of love and adoration. . . . That it was a great delusion to
> think that time set aside for prayer should be different from
> other times, that we were equally obliged to be united to God
> by work in the time assigned to work as by prayer during
> prayer time. That his prayer was simply an awareness of the

presence of God, at which time his soul was oblivious to everything else but love; but that afterward he found no difference. . . .[13]

Many young Christians, reading their New Testaments, have
become increasingly aware that something is missing in our
worship. They are trying to do something about it. With
guitars and improvised songs and informality they are telling
us that "playing church" can deteriorate into a tedious game,
that having Jesus in our hearts is the only true worship. Gradually they are moving the church away from its rigid patterns
into a more fluid style of worship.

Often their effort fails. It shows its immaturity, becomes
self-conscious, wobbly, insipid, and noisy. But sometimes it is
magnificently effective. Recently Winola and I worshiped in a
congregation of two thousand young people who did nothing
but sing Scripture verses for the better part of an hour. They
vocalized softly, harmoniously, without benefit of choir or any
instrument except a single guitar. As we sang with them the
immortal words of the Psalmist, it became apparent that we
were indeed worshiping the Lord in the beauty of holiness.
The abuses of worship in the near and distant past were forgotten. For a memorable span of time we were led in simplicity to the holy hill and given a passing glimpse of the glory of
God in the face of Jesus Christ.

CHAPTER FIFTEEN
The Altar

Then will I go to the altar of God,
to God, my joy and my delight.
I will praise you with the harp,
O God, my God.
—Psalm 43:4

THE VOICE OF THE BELOVED

In its masterly progression our Psalm now approaches a crescendo. We are in the Spirit on the holy mountain, in the court of the temple, and moving toward the sacred altar of God where dwells the Shekinah Glory.[1] For the Psalmist it is an anticipation; for you and me it is perhaps a reality. It is the exquisite moment of moments when time comes to a stop. The perennial human thirst for God is about to be quenched, and the soul stands beside itself with joy.

What a prospect of delight! Instead of ashes, beauty; instead of mourning, the oil of joy; instead of the spirit of heaviness, the garment of praise.[2] Like the Psalmist, we have been through the waves and breakers. We have fed on tears and panted for the streams of water. Our bones have been crushed, our souls disturbed, until it seemed certain God had rejected us.

No more.

Right now we are speaking of a joy the world knows nothing of. Sex, romance, travel, entertainment, ambition, even family affection pale beside the sheer gladness of knowing God and sensing that his love is being poured out into our hearts by the Holy Spirit.

How does one describe it? How does one capture in words that sudden rush of ecstasy, that breath of fragrance blown in from another world, that shivery awareness that God is real, that he is my God, my Father, and knows me and will help me? That he is the true God, the only God, who reigns in truth and righteousness?

As I move toward the altar I don't feel forgiven; that will come later. To be honest, until this moment I was hardly aware of my sins. Only now, as I step into the circle of God's love, do I realize the gulf that separates me from his holiness. A soldier forgets the pain of his wounds when he is reunited with his loved ones; and I have forgotten everything except that I am going to the altar of God, my joy and my delight.

Here the Song of Songs proves its title and its right to be included in the canon of Sacred Scripture, for nowhere else do we find the note of joy in God's presence sounded in just this way:

> The voice of my beloved! Behold, he cometh leaping upon the mountains, skipping upon the hills. . . . Thou hast ravished my heart. . . . I am my beloved's, and my beloved is mine. . . . My beloved is gone down into his garden, to the beds of spices, to feed in the gardens, and to gather lilies.[3]

Sometimes in my reading I find myself melting into that pure love for Jesus that brings me close to tears, and I am once again in the temple of Zion, moving toward the altar. One such moment occurred when I came across the apocryphal "Odes of Solomon" and read such lines as these:

I should not have known how to love the Lord
if he had not loved me
for who is able to grasp the meaning of love
except the one that is loved?

As the sun is the joy to those
who long for its daybreak
so is my joy the Lord
because he is my Sun
and his rays have lifted me up
and his light has dispelled all darkness
from my face.
In him I have been given eyes
to see his holy day.[4]

How dull at such a moment seem all the books on history, doctrine, and church order. I forget whether I am a Presbyterian or Baptist or Pentecostal or Syrian Orthodox. What interests me is Paul's statement that he was caught up to the third heaven.[5] I reach out across the centuries to Bernard of Clairvaux, who wrote,

As honey to the taste, as melody in the ear, as songs of gladness in the heart, so is the Name of Jesus.[6]

My heart is linked with the author of *The Cloud of Unknowing*, who spoke of "some taste of the infinite sweetness." And at last I understand why Thomas Aquinas, having caught something of the ineffable beauty of God, refused to write another line of theology.

But the wine of the altar is heady wine, and it may make us forget that we are earth creatures who need Jesus every day.

Once Billy Graham took part in a television talk show in London that included some well-known British personalities. The host was discussing the current evangelistic crusade in Earls Court and asked—as they always do—"Do all those people who come forward really 'last'?" A prominent actress seated next to him commented, "What if they don't?"

Everyone looked a bit startled, including Graham. She went on, "What if, in all their lives, they have just that one beautiful moment with God as they come and stand at his altar. Isn't that better than nothing?"

I could sympathize with her. Like many others, I have had moments of high feeling when God seemed very close. But behind the actress' sentiment lay a dangerous concept: out of a wasted, selfish life, one redeemed instant. One moment to know God; to be clothed in love, to feel the breath of his Spirit, and behold the unstained radiance of eternity. One romantic moment at the altar—and then what? Jesus indicated that the branch would have to bear fruit or the last state of it would be worse than the first.

Unless we are prepared to receive Jesus as Lord as well as Savior, and seek to serve him daily, we had best stay away from the altar; we can only profane it with such dithering.

THE HARP

"Heaven," said Thomas Campion, "is music." "I will praise you," said the Psalmist, "with the harp." His harp, or lyre, was a small, portable wooden instrument with eight or ten strings. We are told the ancient Hebrews used flutes, pipes, timbrels, trumpets, and other instruments in their religious celebrations.

Music is a natural channel to express one's feelings toward God. Music was born in the heart of God, and whether one is thirsting for him or drinking at his fountain, it's only natural to let music set the mood. In some wonderful and mysterious way music makes us part of the harmony of creation. The Book of Job speaks of the morning stars singing together. Perhaps the universe did not begin with a "big bang" after all; perhaps it began with music.

In the Book of Revelation John records that in his vision he looked out across a sea of glass and saw people standing with harps and singing.[7] We don't know much about the furniture of heaven, but it seems there will be music and musical instruments.

All this is too much for me; I cannot explain it. Music is not my field. I cannot understand how a strain of melody—a simple song about Jesus—will usher a seeker into the presence of God when a cassette library of sermons will leave him cold. Somehow music reaches into the unconscious and plays upon the chords of memory. It can have an astonishing effect upon the personality, and particularly upon the decision-making apparatus.

In his *Republic,* Plato insisted that music is inseparably linked with moral beauty, and a person is never truly musical until he possesses such qualities as loyalty, courage, temperance, and liberality. He claimed that the absence of rhythm and harmony is closely allied to an evil style and evil character. Therefore he attached supreme importance to the musical education of children and demanded that they be exposed only to the noblest of musical influences. Poets, he said, should suit their compositions to "the natural rhythms of a manly and well-regulated life."[8]

What would Plato say about our musical chaos today? No subject in Western culture is so hotly debated. Writing in 1939, Phil Kerr drew a distinction between the hymn and the gospel song.[9] A hymn, he said, is a praise song or a prayer song. A gospel song is a testimony song. The one is addressed to God, the other to people. The one should be sung with reverence, the other with enthusiasm. But over the years Phil Kerr's distinction has been blurred; the line today is not between worship and testimony, but between worship and entertainment. Religious music is being huckstered along with secular music until it is often impossible to tell the difference between them.

At no point is the generation gap wider in North America than in the divergent musical tastes of individuals. Even among Christians we find a gulf. Some, for example, say they find a genuine sense of release and freedom in listening to what is known as "Christian rock." To millions of other Christians, however, such music is a sound imported straight from hell. They are convinced that it undermines character, weakens moral resolve, and destroys the finer sensibilities; that it changes beauty into ugliness and the garment of praise into the spirit of antichrist.

"While we were teaching the children of Africa to sing, 'Yes, Jesus loves me,' " wrote Kerr, "Satanic inspiration was injecting the virus of jungle rhythm into us."[10] I wonder what he would say about disco.

At the other end of the spectrum many churches are guilty
of snobbishness with regard to music. Insisting that "we must
give of our best to the Master," they will not allow gospel
music to be played, much less sung, on their premises.
Nonetheless, they've been known to indulge in classical music
whether sacred or profane, aesthetics seemingly having replaced the devotional spirit as a criterion of worship. Sometimes it is called "tradition." There's nothing wrong with
aesthetics and certainly nothing wrong with tradition. What is
wrong is that worshipers in such churches are deprived of
tunes they learned as children, music which, with lyrics based
on Scripture, could well reorient their lives and lead them to
God.

If the guitar and the drum are responsible for part of our
musical disarray, the organ is perhaps equally guilty. As an
instrument of versatility and power, the organ can render
magnificent tones to the glory of God. But I cannot refrain
from noting some comments of Ira Sankey on the use of the
organ in worship. These words were spoken at a convention of
evangelicals in New York's Hippodrome in 1876, and they
could well apply today:

> A large organ can be played very softly, so that the people's
> voices are not drowned; but you usually find it the case that
> the organ is played so hard as to shake the whole building, and
> to shake the whole people, so that they can hardly sing them-
> selves. I would ask the organist to play very softly, so as to
> have the people led by the organ's tones, and not their atten-
> tion taken up by it. I would rather have a small organ than a
> large one, not to drown the people's voices but simply to
> support them. I don't care if the organ is not heard ten feet
> away, if the choir hear it. What we want is the human voice.
> There is nothing equal to that in the world.[11]

Were we to enter the courts of the temple with the Psalmist
and listen as his hand moves across the strings of his harp, we
would realize that the Psalms were written to be sung. Instead of being overpowered with noise, we would be moved
to worship. Instead of clapping our hands to applaud the entertainment, we would be lifting our hearts in praise to God.

As he sings of the "gladness of his joy" (as he does in this Psalm) we would respond with "Amen. Hallelujah!" And we would thank God for the gift of music.

THE TEST OF HOLINESS

Does going to the altar really make a difference in our lives? Does it improve our characters and lift us above the common level of behavior? To repeat the point: if it doesn't produce, what good is it?

The issue of sanctification has troubled the church for centuries. Our sanctification is God's will—that is clear from Scripture. But it seems when Christians become convinced they are sanctified and holy, they are often extremely difficult to live with. They appear to assume a judgmental role, looking down on the rest of mortals who go bumbling along in their sins. But the rest of mortals, deep in their hearts, are firmly convinced that those who claim to be sanctified are the worst sinners of all. Not just because of their hypocrisy (although that too is suspect), but because of their sanctimonious pride.

It is obvious that when the Psalmist talked about going to the altar of God, he was not thinking of any effort at self-improvement. Yet we cannot get away from the question of character improvement, for if Christianity is not concerned with character, what is it concerned with?

Perhaps we can rephrase our question and ask, not whether persons who commit their lives to Christ become "better," but rather how they would evaluate themselves. Do they think better of themselves after they have received a touch from God?

It is a curious fact that the saints whom the Roman Catholic Church has canonized did not look upon themselves as better than other people, but worse. Many of them spent their days mourning their weakness and lack of character; yet the church decided after their death that they were in fact not only better, but the best.

When Peter came face to face with Holiness, he cried, "Go away from me, Lord; I am a sinful man!"[12] His reaction was authentic. The first lesson the Holy Spirit teaches a lover of

God is that he is no better than anyone else; but often it is the first one forgotten. There is unwritten consensus among most Christians that we understand ourselves to be a cut above the common level. We may not admit it, but we think it.

In a sense it is true! We conduct ourselves as socially responsible citizens. We teach our children to respect the law. We avoid the wrong places and frequent the right places. And all this good behavior does more than just build our self-regard. It gives us an inflated sense of pride and superiority. We conclude that we are Somebody; then we read books by Christian psychologists convincing us that this is a very good thing indeed. Didn't Jesus tell us to love ourselves—or did he?

Somehow we have drifted a long way from Thomas à Kempis, who wrote in his *Imitation of Christ:*

> Why do you wish to esteem yourself above others, when there are many who are wiser and more perfect in the Law of God? If you desire to know or learn anything to your advantage, then take delight in being unknown and unregarded. A true understanding and humble estimate of oneself is the highest and most valuable of all lessons. To take no account of oneself, but always to think well and highly of others is the highest wisdom and perfection. . . . We are all frail; consider none more frail than yourself.[13]

Thomas has a more biblical ring than anything I can find in the self-concept literature. I hear an echo of the apostle Paul:

> As servants of God we commend ourselves in every way: . . . through glory and dishonor, bad report and good report, genuine, yet regarded as impostors; known, yet regarded as unknown; dying, and yet we live on; beaten, and yet not killed; sorrowful, yet always rejoicing; poor, yet making many rich; having nothing, and yet possessing everything.[14]

This kind of commendation makes sense to me as a Christian. The only self-assurance we really need is the inner assurance that God loves us. But since God loves everybody, it is hardly cause for aggressive self-conceit.

If being filled with the Spirit makes some noticeable improvement in our behavior, it is for others and not for us to say so. Don't ask a Christian what going forward to the altar did for him. Ask his wife, his next-door neighbor, his companions at work. The Book of Acts tells us that when Paul and Barnabas returned to Antioch after founding churches in Asia Minor, they did not talk about their adventures, but about what God had done.[15] In our testimonies we need to make that distinction. An enormous amount of bragging is heard in our churches under the guise of "witnessing," yet no one has ever considered pride a sign of sanctification or improved character.

If boasting is not the New Testament way, why should it be ours? If someone asked, "How would you rate yourself on a scale of one to ten?" I would reply, "It would be more accurate if you did the rating." Knowing myself as I do, I would not attempt it.

I have seen God do lovely things in churches: heal hurts, dissolve hostilities, reconcile quarrels. No statistics are needed, for God has nothing to prove. The ministry is not any one person's doing, nor is it the churches'. God's people prepare the altar and the sacrifice; he sends down the fire.

The Psalmist had much to say about his hopes, little about his achievements. He hoped to get to the altar. We're not sure he did. Yet as Harington Evans said, the Psalmist might have gone a thousand times to the tabernacle and never found a thousandth part of the blessing he found in the wilderness.[16] And what a blessing he has been to the millions who have read, studied, and wept over the Forty-second and Forty-third Psalms! God has used him as he has used few human beings.

Are you still skeptical? Then take my hand, and together we will walk up the holy mountain and enter the temple court and approach the altar of God, our joy and our delight. There I will pray with you, and Someone will warm your heart, and you too will say as the Psalmist said so long ago, "O God, my God!" That is holiness.

CHAPTER SIXTEEN

Hope

Why are you downcast, O my soul?
    Why so disturbed within me?
Put your hope in God,
    for I will yet praise him,
the salvation of my face
    and my God."
                          —Psalm 43:5

OUT OF THE DUMPS

Here in a single verse is the whole Bible. All the riches of faith, the distilled essence of truth, the Good News of the Gospel itself, can be drawn from these words. Even though the misery of the human condition (which some three billion people will have no trouble in recognizing) is still with us, we are shown a way to something better.

The word *downcast* has sometimes been translated "exceedingly sorrowful." It has been suggested that Jesus may have been thinking of this verse during his time of spiritual agony in the Garden of Gethsemane. But just as the Resurrection stood behind his Passion, so in this verse we find, in the midst of trial, hope and deliverance. Even before we finish reading it our spirits are raised. Gratitude and praise to God bring the two Psalms to their sublime conclusion.

One of the meanings of heaven is that God saves the best till the last. He does so in this Psalm. But you may have noticed that the words of 43:5 have already appeared twice in Psalm 42, with slight variations. They appear in 42:5 and then with highly significant differences in 42:11 and 43:5. The refrain serves to bind the two Psalms together and thus arranges the flow of thought in a pattern which becomes one of the most beautiful lyrical expressions in all poetry.

But let's look at those variations which the translations sometimes hide. In Psalm 42:5 the Psalmist says literally, "Put your hope in God, for I will yet praise him, *whose face is my salvation.*" In 42:11 and 43:5 the wording is altered: "I will yet praise him, *the salvation of my face, and my God.*"

Alexander of Princeton calls this change "bold and unusual." Martyn Lloyd-Jones says the Psalmist is telling us, "When I really look at God, as I get better, my face gets better also."[1]

It is not unusual for the Bible to speak of God's face being a blessing. In Numbers 6:25-26 occurs the well-known benediction,

> "The Lord make his face shine upon you
>   and be gracious to you;
> the Lord turn his face toward you
>   and give you peace."

But now it is the Psalmist's own face that is blessed. God's face is shining, and the believer's face reflects the light.

What is this shining face of God, if not the Holy Spirit? Just as Jesus Christ was the face of God turned toward us in the days of his flesh, so the Spirit of God, whom our Lord sent, fills that role today. He becomes the "salvation of our face," or as the older version has it, "the health of our countenance."

At this point, says John Trapp, the Psalmist "chideth himself out of the dumps."[2] The "chicken-hearted melancholy,"

as Spurgeon called it, becomes a garden of roses and lilies.[3]
Satan is saying, "This man cannot be damned; I drag him
through perdition, and he comes out praying."[4]

Since this verse was written, how many millions of people
have been helped by this dialogue of a lonely human being
with himself? Here is one case, recorded nearly three hundred years ago by Samuel Clarke of England:

> There was one Alice Benden, who among others was impris-
> oned for religion in Canterbury castle; but after awhile, by the
> bishop's order, she was let down into a deep dungeon where
> none of her friends could come at her. There she was fed with
> an halfpenny bread and a farthing beer a day, neither would
> they allow her any more for her money. Her lodging was upon
> a little straw, between a pair of stocks and a stone wall. This
> made her grievously to bewail and lament her estate, reason-
> ing with herself, why her Lord God did in so heavy a wise
> afflict her, and suffered her thus to be sequestered from the
> sweet society of her loving prison-fellows. In this extremity of
> misery, and in the midst of these dolorous mournings she
> continued, till on a night, repeating that of the Psalmist: 'Why
> art thou so heavy, O my soul? And why art thou so cast down
> within me? Still trust in God,' and, 'God's right hand can
> change all this,' she received comfort in the midst of her sor-
> rows, and so continued joyful to the time of her release.[5]

Spurgeon said, "This verse, like the singing of Paul and Silas,
looses chains and shakes prison walls."[6] It did not shake the
wall of Alice Benden's dungeon, but it gave her victory over
it. And for us that is even more hopeful.

Alexander and others have pointed out that while the
translation, "Why are you downcast?" (or "Why are you cast
down?") is passive, the original Hebrew is in active voice, so
that the phrase should be rendered, "Why do you bow yourself down?" or "Why do you deject yourself?"[7] Delitzsch says
that the Hebrew word *tishtochachi* means to bow oneself very
low, to sit upon the ground like a mourner, and to bend
oneself downward; to utter a deep groan and mumble to oneself.[8] It is a vivid picture of a human being soaked in his own
misery and feeling desperately sorry for himself.

Now the Psalmist is saying to himself, "Quit it, you.

Enough of this blethering!" He knows that giving in to his gnawing and desponding grief is churning up his inner self and getting him nowhere. He knows, too, whose fault it is. The devil didn't make him do it. Neither God nor Satan is afflicting him; he is laying this trouble on himself. But that doesn't make it any less trouble.

The expression "disturbed within me" (or as the older versions have it, "disquieted within me") apparently signifies more than uneasiness. It suggests a noisy restlessness, violent agitation, a "roaring" and a "moaning" like the tossing waves of the ocean. Some years ago I wrote a little verse:

> Lord, if I dig a pit for others
> let me fall into it;
> but if I dig it for myself,
> give me sense enough to walk around.[9]

There comes a time when we simply have to stop making things hard for ourselves. God does not cast down or cast off his children, but we can do it to ourselves. And that is no way out of the dumps. We'll have to find a better way.

THIRD AND LONG

The southern coast of England is lined in places with steep, rugged cliffs, three hundred to five hundred feet in height. Over the centuries, at certain seasons of the year, residents of the coastal area have made a living by gathering a carrot-like root called samphire and collecting eggs of seabirds that nest in the rocks.

To reach the eggs in past years was a hazardous occupation. A more daring hunter would drive an iron bar into the ground near the cliff edge, strap a basket to his back, and lower himself over the precipice with a rope until he reached the ledges where the nests were. Once he found solid footing, he would fill his basket and then climb back hand over hand to the lip of the cliff, where others would pull him to safety.

The story is told that one man went out early and managed to lower himself a good distance down the cliff, where he gained a narrow ledge of a rock. Because this ledge was overhung by the cliff, he could only get there by swinging in; but he made it safely. Then while he was removing his basket he accidentally let go the rope. It swung away and out of reach. Realizing his plight, he called for help, but no one was around and his cries went unheard.

The man now sized up his prospects. The alternatives were spending an indefinite time on the ledge, falling to the rocks, or catching the rope. But the rope had swung far out, and in its returning arc it did not quite reach the ledge. Furthermore, he noted that each movement was shorter than the one before.

"If I stay here," he thought, "I may be rescued and I may not. That rope is one sure chance to save myself. If I wait, it will be beyond my reach. It is nearer now than it ever will be again. What can I lose?"

The basket and the eggs were forgotten. As the rope swung toward him he sprang from the ledge and caught it in his grasp in midair, climbed up, and went home.[10]

As long as the Psalmist talked about his problems, you and I were with him. He was, we say, speaking for many people; but now he is all through letting his fears run his life. He sees a rope and is reaching out. "Why are you casting yourself down?" he asks himself. "Nothing is down there but rocks. Put your hope in God." The time of groaning and mumbling and hand-wringing is past. No longer is he sprawled in the dumps; he is standing erect with his hand outstretched. There is hope and there is help.

God's face is turned toward him, shining upon him, at least for the moment. It is nearer now perhaps than it ever will be again. To wait is to risk the loss of everything. He responds in faith, knowing that his problem is not solved and he is still a great distance from his goal. A point to remember is that human assistance is not around; he is on his own. Nevertheless he is confident, for he is now resting in God's promise and can say three times over, "I will yet praise him."

John Brodie, the former San Francisco Forty-niners football player who is now a sports commentator, recently described a typical situation in a professional game. "It's third down and long yardage," he said. "You're the quarterback, you look to the bench for guidance, and do you know what the coaches are doing? They're counting the house, is what they are doing. Which means you're on your own."[11]

And that's where you are: on your own. It's third and long, and the people you looked to for advice are counting the house. Now what? Would you say (to change the figure) that you are still standing on the ledge and watching the rope? That ledge would seem to be getting crowded. For many years I stood there, and it's not the most satisfying way to live the Christian life. Having committed my heart to Jesus Christ, having accepted the authority of Scripture, I was engaged in an international ministry of evangelism through literature. It did not occur to me to look for something better in my personal spiritual life, because I was persuaded that there wasn't anything better.

My friends assured me, "Once you have come to Christ, the rest of it is simply yielding. You keep on yielding different areas of your life to God as he shows you where you are lacking." But I have found that yielding won't get you off the ledge; there has to be a rope! And what if you won't yield and don't feel like yielding? What if you receive guidance from God and man and then don't follow it? What then? What, indeed! For that's where I was, minutely righteous, curiously unloving, hung up on my hang-ups, saved (if you can call existing on a ledge being saved) with an empty basket and no rope. I was just another evangelical cheating myself out of the blessing of God.

Perhaps that is why in North America alone born-again Christians can number thirty or forty or fifty million and yet have such little effect on the body politic. We cannot turn society around because we cannot turn ourselves around. Instead of crying "Halt!" we blend into the coloration of our environment. We're willing to die for our country if called upon, but when it comes to our cultural drift—our moral skid that is making Sodom and Gomorrah look like DisneyWorld —we hesitate to resist it because (1) we like it somewhat, (2) we feel no great urge to resist, and (3) if we did resist, we would sound like a voice crying in the wilderness.

With respect to the first two points, we should obviously

either overhaul our attitudes or drop the label "evangelical"; but we intend to do neither, because of the third point. The situation calls for help from beyond us. Let's take a moment and look again at that biblical expression, "a voice crying in the wilderness."

The voice belonged to John the Baptist, who made as large a dent in history as any man of his age or any age. With all that has been written about John, not too much attention has been paid to the main purpose of his ministry.

Ruth Paxson, for many years a Bible teacher in China, says, "In two wonderful proclamations, John the Baptist declared the entire scope of Christ's work." His first proclamation was "Behold, the Lamb of God, who takes away the sin of the world!"[12] John was interpreting the future ministry of Jesus of Nazareth. By calling Jesus "the Lamb of God," he was pointing to the Cross, to the vicarious sacrifice that would atone for our sins and restore our fellowship with God our Father. John's words enabled the future church to understand the meaning of our Lord's coming, suffering, and death. He foresaw what it would be, the crucifixion of the Just for the unjust in obedience to the Father's will.

The second proclamation, says Miss Paxson, was, "The one who sent me to baptize with water . . . is he who will baptize with the Holy Spirit."[13] Those words prepare us to understand the meaning of Pentecost. They pointed to a time when the followers of Jesus would be given a Guide, a Friend, a Counselor, an Advocate who would bless the church as it sought to serve humanity and await its Bridegroom's return; and who would come and fill us with God's love as our Lord commanded us to be filled.

One day in 1972 under the ministry of friends I prayed to be filled with the Holy Spirit. In the months that followed I learned that we Christians don't have to live lives that are wistful, disappointed, lonely, and bored. We don't have to wear a hallelujah-mask or disguise our feelings with pious nothings. We don't have to cover up our fears. Our churches don't have to be redesigned into "fellowships" and places of entertainment. There *is* something better.

Even though we may not be spiritually gifted in any spectacular way, we can be spiritually filled. We can know contentment and praise and joy and peace and love. Our voice crying in the wilderness will be heard, just as John's was. We can say to a careless world, "Not that way—this way!" And because we say it in love, people will hear. The Spirit will use us, because the Spirit is love.

The Psalmist found himself in a situation that floored him. His back was on the canvas, but he did not throw in the towel. Did he get all he asked for? We don't know. What we do know is that he longed for God for his own sake; not for what his longing would get out of God, but for what it would have in God. Alexander Maclaren says that at the end of Psalm 43 "he already tastes the rapture of the joy that will then flood his heart." He adds a striking phrase: "It is the prerogative of faith to make pictures drawn by memory pale beside those painted by hope."[14]

Whatever was God's answer to the Psalmist's prayer, you and I have something even better awaiting us, if only we knew it.[15] What was to the Psalmist an expectation and a hope has become to us a realization through the cross and resurrection of Jesus Christ and the ministry of his Spirit.

JACOB'S WELL

It was a favorite practice of Evangelist Dwight L. Moody to trace single words through the Bible. He did it even before he knew about concordances. Earlier in this chapter I remarked that the closing words of Psalm 43 are sure to lift our spirits. Let us now examine more carefully that single word *lift,* for it appears in a number of places in the Old and New Testaments. Here are some of them:

> I will exalt you, O Lord,
>> for you lifted me out of the depths.

> Bring joy to your servant,
>> for to you, O Lord,
>> I lift up my soul.

> I lift up my eyes to you,
>> to you whose throne is in heaven.

Let the morning bring me word of your unfailing love,
for I have put my trust in you.
Show me the way I should go,
for to you I lift up my soul.[16]

You who bring good tidings to Jerusalem,
lift up your voice with a shout,
lift it up, do not be afraid;
say to the towns of Judah,
"Here is your God!"[17]

Let us examine our ways and test them,
and let us return to the Lord.
Let us lift up our hearts and our hands
to God in heaven. . . .[18]

"When these things begin to take place, stand up and lift up
your heads, because your redemption is drawing near."[19]

"I when I am lifted up from the earth, will draw all men to
myself."[20]

And finally,

Humble yourselves before the Lord, and he will lift you up.[21]

What has this review of Scripture taught us? We are to lift up
our souls to God, and our heads and our eyes and our hearts
and our hands and our voices, but *not* our selves. On the
contrary, we are to lower ourselves and lift up Jesus. "He
must increase," said John, "but I must decrease."[22] That is
hardly the principle on which the world operates. We're more
familiar with the procedure suggested by W. S. Gilbert's
satirical lines:

If you wish in the world to advance,
Your merits you're bound to enhance,
You must stir it and stump it,
And blow your own trumpet,
Or, trust me, you haven't a chance![23]

In such an environment (and Sir William is perhaps not too
wide of the mark), the only person who can humble himself is
the person who is sure of himself. In some way or other he has
been to the altar. He can accept praise with graciousness and
criticism with equanimity. He has climbed off his pedestal,

has stopped reaching for self-concepts, and is looking for something better.

What might that be?

A person thirsting for God does not necessarily feel holy; nor does he feel depraved or condemned or penitent. He simply feels thirsty. Only after he begins to drink from the Spring does he gain an inkling into what he is searching for. Once he stops asking "Where is God?" and starts saying with the Psalmist "O God, my God!" his universe gradually comes together. He learns about sin and forgiveness—lessons he once knew, perhaps, but which have been brought afresh to his mind. He swaps his self-esteem for grace and his self-worth for gratitude. He trades in his self-hoisting apparatus for the Lord's lifting-up mercy. And he escapes the fate of a Ping-Pong ball, batted back and forth between pride and humility, by simply giving his life away to other people.

The Psalmist ends his Psalm by singing, "I will yet praise him, the Savior of my face, and my God." One hopeful sign of our day is that people are finding through the therapy of praise that God can still accomplish mighty things. In this discovery the church owes a debt to its young people. They have led the way in congregation after congregation, bringing to the consciousness of the average jaded worshiper the sheer joy and delight of lifting up one's voice in praise to God. Just by sounding the note of praise, the Psalmist here points to something better.

Suppose you roll up to your favorite gas station, hoping that the attendant will allow you to fill your tank. Someone you do not know is standing by the pump. You order, "Fill it up, please."

He says, "If you will use the fuel that I offer you, you will never need a refill, but you will have enough to last a lifetime." You notice that he is not a driver and has no vehicle. Is he a salesman? Is he a plant? You become suspicious and go looking for the manager.

A Samaritan women once came to a well outside Sychar, expecting to draw water. A Jewish stranger was seated there. He asked her for a drink; she demurred. He then told her he could give her Living Water that would cause her never to thirst again. She too reacted suspiciously: "The well is deep and you have nothing to draw with."[24]

It isn't that our churches have empty tanks or empty pots; it's *we* who are empty. Moreover, we are suspicious. We have heard the old religious clichés too many times.

But suppose a curious thing were to happen to us while we are reading our way through the Bible. Suppose in the middle of the Psalms we find a man who said that he, too, was empty. He was thirsting for God, for the living God, and he asked God for light and truth, and God sent them both in the form of hope.

That is the message of these Psalms. They were not composed in the Emerald City of Oz. They were written in a place of desolation where there was no altar, only pain and discouragement. But instead of inquiring of his fears, the Psalmist chose to inquire of God. He took a dark providence and turned it into hope; and as we know, hope always points beyond itself. So when the Psalmist told himself, "Hope in God," he was really pointing to Israel's hope, the Son of David, the Messiah—the Jewish stranger seated by the well.

When we reach the New Testament we find the message more explicit. We are to vacate the premises of the self, to become empty vessels so that we can be filled with the Holy Spirit. If we do, Jesus will quench our thirst and make us into vessels of love, from whom streams of blessing will flow to help a troubled world.

That's something better. That's what we want.

CHAPTER SEVENTEEN
Selah

I urge you, brothers and sisters,
by our Lord Jesus Christ and
by the love of the Spirit. . . .
—Romans 15:30

THE PROMISE

We have finished our tour of two magnificent Psalms. We have tracked our man through desert and deep water, through harassment and soul agony. In the devil's ballpark he

Mystery surrounds the exact meaning of the word *Selah*, which occurs seventy-one times in the Psalms. Some have conjectured that it marks a rise in the musical accompaniment. I like the interpretation of my friend Paul Anderson, who says it means simply: "What do you know about that!"

has touched all the bases. The chief impression we have come away with is still a *yearning*. Our Psalmist is reaching out, thirsting, panting, in a mighty longing after God. Perhaps that's why we love him so, for we are with him.

In some ways our situation is unchanged from those ancient times. Satan still harasses us. The comforts of affluence are pleasant, but life today does not seem to spare us either desert or deep water. Every one of our churches lies in the vale of tears. On the international scene our future looks uneasy and in many respects grim.

Yet to most of us things appear different from the way they looked to the Psalmist. We're not weeping in exile. We can actually go to the house of God with the voice of joy and praise; he couldn't. Our churches are open and protected and free. Many of them, having repudiated what Tozer calls "a servile imitation of the world,"[1] are proclaiming the whole counsel of God. We can thank the Lord for that.

And something else has changed. Have you noticed that while the Psalms were written under the inspiration of the Holy Spirit, his name is seldom mentioned in them? Many books have been written to explain the differing roles of the Holy Spirit in the Old and New Testaments, and I do not intend to add another. I merely want to affirm that there is such a difference.

Beginning with the birth and baptism of Jesus, a significant turning took place in the Holy Spirit's ministry. Certain messianic passages in the Old Testament point to that change:

> "Do not be afraid, O Jacob, my servant. . . .
> For I will pour water on the thirsty land,
>   and streams on the dry ground;
> I will pour out my Spirit on your offspring,
>   and my blessing on your descendants."[2]

> "I will sprinkle clean water on you, and you will be clean. . . .
> I will give you a new heart and put a new spirit in you; I will remove from you your heart of stone and give you a heart of flesh. And I will put my Spirit in you and move you to follow my decrees. . . ."[3]

Jesus, after telling his disciples that he would ask his Father to give them "another Counselor," said at the close of his ministry, "I am going to send you what my Father has promised."[4]

Since the Holy Spirit had been around since the beginning of creation, it becomes very important to us to understand what Jesus meant by that word *promise.* In the context of Scripture the word is usually associated with God; it refers to something God said he would do. He would make Israel "his people"; he would give them the "promised land"; he would bless the families of earth through Abraham; he would give his people rest; he would send a Messiah to deliver them.

In the New Testament the promises of God include an eternal inheritance, a place in the Kingdom, and the return of Jesus Christ.[5] But now we come to the promise I would like us especially to consider: what Jesus called "the promise of the Father," namely, the gift of the Holy Spirit.

THE DELIVERY

In Psalm 77, a Psalm of Asaph, we find a familiar complaint:

> "Will the Lord reject us forever? . . .
> Has his promise failed for all time?"

The author of Hebrews, after calling the roll of Old Testament worthies, says, "These were all commended for their faith, *yet none of them received what had been promised,* God having foreseen *something better* for us. . . ."[7]

Notice that the Old and New Testaments agree that an unfulfilled relationship existed to this point between God and his children. Something that was expected had been kept back. With this in mind, I ask you to read the following New Testament passages:

> "If you then, though you are evil, know how to give good gifts to your children, how much more will your Father in heaven give the Holy Spirit to those who ask him? . . ."

> "I am going to send you what my Father has promised; but stay in the city until you have been clothed with power from on high."[8]

"Do not leave Jerusalem, but wait for the gift my Father promised, which you have heard me speak about. For John baptized with water, but in a few days you will be baptized with the Holy Spirit. . . ."

"He [Christ] has received from the Father the promise of the Holy Spirit and has poured out what you now see and hear. . . ."

"You will receive the gift of the Holy Spirit. The promise is for you and for your children. . . ."[9]

He redeemed us . . . so that by faith we might receive the promise of the Spirit.[10]

Having believed, you were sealed in him [Christ] with the Holy Spirit of promise.[11]

Add to them this verse from Hebrews that is usually associated with the Lord's return, but notice how it might apply to a Christian who knows he is not filled with the Spirit, yet would like to be:

You need to persevere so that when you have done the will of God, you will receive what he has promised. For in just a very little while, He who is coming will come and will not delay.[12]

A promise *given* is not the same as a promise *kept*. What happened in the Upper Room, as reported in Acts 2, was more than a promise to the church. It was a delivery, the "thing itself." When Jesus went to Jerusalem, John tells us, "the Spirit was not yet."[13] But in that Upper Room everything changed, which is why Pentecost is called the birthday of the church. The Spirit descended. Pentecost was a promise kept.

David Wilkerson says that the baptism of the Holy Spirit was "a baptism of love that God poured out on the whole church at Pentecost." The Book of Acts tells of a Christian community suddenly set aglow with zeal and joy and love. For the first time, it seems, God opened the possibility of the life in Christ. Unless I am completely mistaken, this means that the Pentecost experience is something each Christian is to undergo himself if he is to know the "something better" that God has promised.

God's sovereign ways are hidden in mystery. Just how and

when Pentecost is recapitulated in the believer is not for me to say. It may come at commitment, it may come later; but that it comes is the surest thing I know.

THE 'TWEEN-DECKS

Back in the Depression days (1933, to be exact) I shipped out to sea in the U.S. Merchant Marine. I served as deckboy on a sugar freighter making the triangle run between San Francisco, Puget Sound, and Hawaii. One of my tasks was to sweep the 'tween-decks, a large, shallow storage area that reeked of old straw and stale raw sugar. It was located between the main deck and the hold.

Retrospectively I can see that in my later Christian life, I spent many years sweeping out the 'tween-decks. People in such a pass are neither enjoying life on deck in the fresh air, nor mucking about in bilgewater; they can claim neither victory nor total defeat. But take my word for it, the 'tween-decks is not a pleasant place.

By the year 1971, after many years in the church and a long personal struggle, I had concluded that it was impossible for me to live the Christian life. The Psalmist put my viewpoint succinctly:

> Such knowledge is too wonderful for me,
> too lofty for me to attain.[14]

Attending services, reading the Bible, and praying were not enough to pry me out of my rut. Pentecost seemed merely an event in church history—important, perhaps, but remote. I was what they call a "carnal Christian," a semi-sanctified sinner, neither on the high road nor the low but floundering, in John Oxenham's phrase, on the misty flats.[15]

People in this puzzling spiritual condition have no problem believing in God or honoring the Lord Jesus Christ. If we are guilty of promoting self under the guise of glorifying Christ, many times we're not aware of it until someone tells us; and people seldom do. Meanwhile our allegiance to our Lord is fixed and our love is real. It just doesn't work.

We walk out of church and get into the car, and five minutes later we are in an argument. We rise from our knees after prayer, and in two minutes we are upset by a telephone call. After reading a chapter, we close our Bible and realize we have not been feeding on the Word but simply taking an aspirin.

As I look back, it is evident that I didn't have the equipment to handle life. Despite my mature years and academic studies, difficult people were too much for me. I couldn't cope with them. The ordinary level of Christian living did not provide me with the resources to deal with emergencies. I lacked the essential qualities to overcome obstacles and emerge victorious.

The result was that even though I held my job successfully and my home did not fall apart, I remained below the line of happiness and contentment. No thought of abandoning Christ or Christianity crossed my mind; I was merely resigned to

> Heigh-dy, heigh-dy
> Misery me, lackadaydee.[16]

To a person living that kind of life, the filling of the Holy Spirit comes as a stupendous, earth-shattering revelation. Now for the first time he sees the Christian life working smoothly. He is pervaded by a generous supply of love, with more to draw on. He is given patience beyond his "boiling point." The foot of the line becomes more attractive than the head. Prayer is now a love tryst. The Bible is alive and exciting and—to his astonishment—applicable to his problems. Instead of being a disappointment, life becomes a blessing; instead of a thorn, a boon.

The question naturally arises, How does one come into this happy state? And it must be stated that while different churches approach the subject differently, there are no "how-to" manuals on being filled with the Spirit.

Let's suppose you have unexpectedly been left a piece of property. You have not seen it, but you drive out to take possession of it. When you arrive you find the place littered with debris and trash and bits of junk. You then return in a borrowed pickup, load it with the trash, and make a trip to— where? To use a polite word, you make a trip to the landfill.

Before the Spirit moves in and takes possession, comes the

unloading and emptying. The ego is dropped off. Self-love is dropped off. Status-seeking is dropped off. Number One is left, not at the foot of the cross, but nailed to it. "I am crucified with Christ." My sin problem is dealt with, and since I have now done the will of God, I am ready to receive the love he has promised. So much for the "how-to."

But aren't there other things to be done? Of course there are, but we don't "up and do them." Once the self is removed and the Holy Spirit is invited in, he takes over. He gives directions and carries them out. He creates the opportunities, issues the invitations, promotes the work. If there is to be restitution, he arranges it and tells us how to go about it. If there is to be a reestablishing of relationships, he sets it up. Oh, there are things for us to do, all right; we simply follow his leading.

One of the biggest mistakes a lover of Jesus can make in his spiritual life is to imagine that because our Lord went to Golgotha, we don't have to go there. Because he was crucified for us, we don't have to be crucified. Our sins are "under the blood" and our salvation is settled for eternity, so now we can let our egos flourish like a green bay tree and the Holy Spirit will help us.

Don't you believe it.

As long as the Christian is operating on self-love and concentrating on a good self-image, the Spirit of God will leave him alone. As long as he is filled with other spirits—lust, greed, fear, envy, pride, hostility, selfish ambition—he cannot be filled with God's Spirit.

God will allow us to run our lives if we so choose. He will permit our churches to conduct their own programs, even to turning the house of God into a poor man's golf club without the fairways or the bar—or the prayer meeting. But he will reserve his Spirit for those who come panting and thirsting for Living Water.

THE BROKEN SNARE

It is a beautiful thing to be filled with what the apostle Paul calls "the love of the Spirit."[17] It is like finding God all over again. It's like taking a voyage to the moon and looking back and seeing our fragile planet, as it were, through the compassionate eyes of him who created it. The sight of it fills our eyes with tears. We want to love everybody.

Why, we ask, should language, culture, skin color, or past bitter memories spoil our life on this little globe? We have so short a time. Why can't we trust each other? Don't we all hurt in the same places? What good is revenge? Whom did it ever help? It's such a tiny ball, this earth! We long to seize a bullhorn and shout across the outer space:

> How good and pleasant it is
> when brothers live together in unity![18]

But we are not on the moon; we're very much on the sinful earth. And while our Psalmist has brought us a long way, we need a fresh guide for what lies ahead of us. Paul tells us, "Be filled with the Spirit."[19] But for many of us the real question is still, "How do I go about it? What am I supposed to do? Tell me the first step."

Here we go again! A major premise of this book is that there isn't any first step—if anything, there is a step backward. Harold J. Ockenga expresses it well: "In order to be filled with the Spirit we must meet God's conditions. To begin with, we confess to God that we are *not* filled with the Spirit."[20]

In other words, we recognize our situation for what it is without touching it up with explanations and exonerations. We drop out of the Easter parade—or better, masquerade—and accept the fact that we're no better than anyone else (a fact which everyone else has already accepted.)

Now we're getting somewhere. And when we touch bottom, like Hopeful in *Pilgrim's Progress*, we find that it is sound. Already the Spirit of God is helping us. As Dr. Ockenga says, "Our infirmities, our frailness, our impotencies, our failures, our reticence, all have their antidote in him."

If there is something better in the Christian life—and there is—it is because Jesus promised it from the hand of the

Father. But it's more than an individual matter; the Holy Spirit is also Lord of the church. So what is the Spirit saying to the churches of our day?

I am no prophet, but I believe he is telling us to slow down the evangelical carousel. He is warning us that our razzle-dazzle is not taking the church into the world, it is taking the world into the church. A long time passed before North America came to accept the evangelical community; let's not destroy our new position of respect by irresponsible behavior and slick showmanship. There is more to evangelizing than excitement, more to communion than communication.

The Spirit of God is also telling us, I believe, to move out of our sanctuaries into the stream of national and international life. The method is evangelism, and the stakes are the future of humanity. For too long the world has been imbibing Western decadence until it believes that we have little to offer apart from our technology. The recent events created by virulent anti-Americanism have, it is true, evoked some signs of vitality in the United States. But anger and threats of reprisal are only temporary stomach relief for a society glutted with discontent. The solution lies with the message Jesus Christ gave to his church. The poured-out love of heaven is the healing balm our earth cities need.

The whole question of "something better" comes down finally to the dimensions of our Psalmist, as a matter between God and the soul. The New Testament tells us that God provides that something in love, and that he is here and available. We can call upon him and he will respond. Why not? Doesn't God want us to love? Isn't that why he made us? Why else are we on this planet?

A Psalm of David says,

> We have escaped like a bird
> out of the fowler's snare;
> the snare has been broken,
> and we have escaped.[21]

Perhaps right now you have the feeling of being trapped. If so, try moving around a little; test what is holding you. It may be that while you were waiting and hoping, the Holy Spirit quietly has taken care of your problem. Your trap is already sprung and broken. See if it isn't so—that God heard your prayer and you are free. Can you believe it after so long? Hallelujah! Now is the time to escape the fowler's snare and fly away. Now comes the Joy, Joy, Joy, Joy.

But don't forget to come back. Jesus needs you.

Bibliographical Note

A number of the standard commentaries on the Psalms, as well as special volumes, were consulted in the course of preparing these chapters.

Earlier commentators whose works were reviewed included J. A. Alexander, C. A. Briggs (International Critical Commentary), John Calvin, T. K. Cheyne, Adam Clarke, A. Cohen, J. E. Cumming, Franz Delitzsch, David Dickson, Joseph S. Exell, E. W. Hengstenberg, Matthew Henry, Ralph W. Keeler, A. F. Kirkpatrick, John Peter Lange, John R. MacDuff, Alexander Maclaren (The Expositor's Bible), F. B. Meyer, C. B. Moll, G. Campbell Morgan, Joseph Parker, J. J. Stewart Perowne, G. Rawlinson (Pulpit Commentary), W. Graham Scroggie, Charles Simeon, Charles H. Spurgeon, and M. R. Vincent.

More recent commentators and other writers consulted were Edyth Sage Armstrong, William Barclay, Rabbi William G. Braude, Stuart Briscoe, Charles J. Callan, Mary Ellen Chase, Arthur G. Clarke, Mitchell Dahood (Anchor Bible), Edwin L. Groenhoff, George S. Gunn, Arthur Emerson Harris, David A. Hubbard, Marion M. Hull, Derek Kidner (Tyndale Commentaries), Herbert C. Leupold, C. S. Lewis, D. Martyn Lloyd-Jones, J. A. Motyer, W. O. E. Oesterley, Erling C. Olsen, E. Bendor Samuel, Ray C. Stedman, Jane T. Stoddart, William R. Taylor (Interpreter's Bible), Mark van Doren and Maurice Samuel, and Artur Weiser.

In the Notes may be found direct quotations from these works as well as from other volumes upon which I drew freely for many of the ideas expressed in these pages.

Notes

CHAPTER ONE: "On the Run"

[1]Most commentators on this verse prefer the feminine (*hind*, or as we would say, *doe*) to the masculine (*hart* or *stag*). They tell us that while the Hebrew noun is masculine, the verb (*pants*) is feminine, as is the word for *soul*. The NIV's *deer* solves the problem nicely. For Appian's comment on snakes, see Adam Clarke's *Commentary* (1810-26), *in loc.*

[2]A. F. Kirkpatrick, *The Book of Psalms* (Cambridge: The University Press, 1910), p. li.

[3]Alexander Maclaren, *The Book of Psalms*, The Expositor's Bible (London: Hodder and Stoughton, 1903), 2:44.

[4]John 7:37.

[5]Joel 2:28-29.

[6]Acts 2:16. Cf. E. M. Blaiklock, *The Acts of the Apostles*, Tyndale New Testament Commentaries (Grand Rapids: Eerdmans, 1975), p. 59.

[7]Matthew 5:6.

[8]Proverbs 20:27.

[9]Maclaren, *The Book of Psalms*, 2:43.

[10]*The Confessions of Augustine in Modern English*, tr. by Sherwood E. Wirt (Grand Rapids: Zondervan, 1977), p. 4.

[11]Lady Julian of Norwich, *Revelations of Divine Love* (London: Methuen, 1911), p. 12.

[12]Perry Miller, *The New England Mind in the Seventeenth Century* (Cambridge, Mass.: Harvard University Press, 1953), p. 3.

[13]By permission of *Fortune* magazine, New York, NY 10020.

[14]Pascal, *Pensées*, 425. Author's translation from the French.

CHAPTER TWO: "Thirst"

[1]Motyer's comment appears in *The New Bible Commentary*, rev. ed. (Grand Rapids: Eerdmans, 1970), p. 478.

[2]Isaiah 20:2-4.

[3]Rabia al-Adawiyya. Cf. Sherwood E. Wirt and Kersten Beckstrom, eds., *Living Quotations for Christians* (New York: Harper & Row, 1974), no. 3508.

[4]From Wirt, *Confessions of Augustine*, p. 125.

[5]Thomas à Kempis, *The Imitation of Christ*, tr. by Sherley-Price (London: Penguin, 1975), book 3, ch. 5, p. 98.

[6]*The Life of Teresa of Jesus* (autobiography), tr. by E. Allison Peers (Garden City, N.Y.: Image Books, 1960), ch. 11, pp. 125-28.

[7]Amy Carmichael, *Edges of His Ways* (London: SPCK, 1955).

[8]Wirt and Beckstrom, *Living Quotations for Christians*, no. 1163.

[9]R. A. Torrey, *How to Pray* (Chicago: Bible Institute Colportage Assn., 1900), p. 32.

[10]From "St. Paul" in F. W. H. Myers, *Collected Poems* (London: Macmillan, 1921).

[11]Wirt and Beckstrom, *Living Quotations for Christians*, no. 1163.

[12]Matthew 5:6.

CHAPTER THREE: "Where Is He?"

[1]John Baillie, *Our Knowledge of God* (London: Oxford University Press, 1949), pp. 123-24.

[2]Romans 11:33.

[3]Martin Luther, *Commentary on Paul's Epistle to the Galatians*, ch. 1:3.

[4]C. S. Lewis interview, published in *Decision* magazine (October-November 1963) and in Lewis, *God in the Dock: Essays on Theology and Ethics* (Grand Rapids: Eerdmans, 1970), p. 265.

[5]Ezekiel 18:23.

[6]Amos 5:14.

[7]Isaiah 55:1–3.

[8]Psalm 80:4–5.

[9]Cf. Richard Quebedeaus, *The Worldly Evangelicals* (San Francisco: Harper & Row, 1978), part III.

[10]Jeremiah 9:1.

[11]Matthew 5:4.

[12]Wirt, *Confessions of Augustine*, p. 117.

[13]Wirt and Beckstrom, *Living Quotations for Christians*, no. 1244.

[14]Hebrews 2:10.

[15]Colossians 1:24.

[16]1 Peter 5:10.

[17]1 Clement 5 (addressed to the Corinthian Church, 96 A.D.). Author: Clement of Rome, d. c. 101 A.D.

[18]2 Corinthians 11:26–27.

CHAPTER FOUR: "How It Was"

[1]Psalm 84:1-2.

[2]Psalm 122:1.

[3]Psalm 68:24-27, 35.

[4]Psalm 48:9-10.

CHAPTER FIVE: "Remembering"

[1]Mount Mizar, mentioned only here in the Bible, has been subject to much scholarly speculation, but its locality and significance are apparently lost in antiquity. The word *mizar* itself means "smallness." Some effort has been made to associate it with Mount Zion. Carl Armerding thinks it may be prophetic of the "little hill" of Calvary (*Psalms in a Minor Key* [Chicago: Moody Press, 1973], p. 83).

[2]Exodus 3:1; Acts 7:23, 29-30.

[3]Joshua 7:6-7.
[4]1 Samuel 1:5-6, 10.
[5]1 Kings 19:4.
[6]2 Kings 5:1ff.
[7]Luke 7:11-13.
[8]Luke 5:2-5.
[9]Mark 5:25-26.
[10]Mark 10:46.
[11]John 5:5-7.
[12]Acts 12:4-6.
[13]Acts 27:29-33.
[14]*Los Angeles Times* (6 December 1978).
[15]1 Samuel 30:6, King James Version.
[16]*Decision* magazine (December 1960), p. 11.
[17]George A. Barrois, ed., *Pathways of the Inner Life* (Indianapolis: Bobbs Merrill, 1956), p. 149.

CHAPTER SIX: "Deep"

[1]Émile Cailliet, *The Clue to Pascal* (Philadelphia: Westminster, 1943), pp. 67–68.
[2]Genesis 1:2. Cf. Ray Stedman, *Folk Psalms of Faith* (Glendale, Calif.: Regal, 1973), p. 139.
[3]Proverbs 3:20.
[4]Wirt, *Confessions of Augustine*, pp. 46, 95.
[5]Romans 11:33.
[6]A. W. Tozer, *The Pursuit of God* (Harrisburg: Christian Publications, 1948), p. 18.
[7]Luke 11:9.
[8]Revelation 2:7.
[9]Psalm 14:2-3. Compare these lines with Lance Morrow's description of current social conditions in his "Time Essay" (*Time* magazine, September 10, 1979; by permission): "The case [for Western decadence] might be argued thus: the nation's pattern is moral and social failure, embellished by hedonism. The work ethic is nearly dead. . . . Bureaucracies keep cloning themselves. Resources vanish. Education fails to educate. The system of justice collapses into a parody of justice. An underclass is trapped, half out of sight, while an opulent traffic passes overhead. Religion gives way to narcissistic self-improvement cults. Society fattens its children on junk food and then permits them to be enlisted in pornographic films. The nation subdivides into a dozen drug cultures—the alcohol culture, the cocaine culture, the heroin culture, the Valium culture, the amphetamine culture, and combinations thereof. Legal abortions and the pervasive custom of contraception suggest a society so chary of its future that it has lost its will to perpetuate itself."
[10]Tozer, *The Pursuit of God*, p. 15.
[11]Barrois, *Pathways of the Inner Life*, pp. 256-57.

CHAPTER SEVEN: "A Song"

[1]Theodore M. Greene, "Christianity and Its Secular Alternatives" in *The Christian Answer*, ed. by H. P. Van Dusen (New York: Scribners, 1945), pp. 51-53.
[2]Psalm 89:1, King James Version.
[3]Hebrews 11:1.
[4]Psalm 119:105.
[5]Quoted in Miles J. Stanford, *Principles of Spiritual Growth* (Lincoln, Neb.: Back to the Bible, 1977), p. 8.
[6]Greene, "Christianity and Its Secular Alternatives," p. 76.
[7]Warren W. Wiersbe, comp., *The Best of A. W. Tozer* (Grand Rapids: Baker, 1978), pp. 166, 170.
[8]Romans 8:28.
[9]Galatians 5:6.
[10]John 13:35.
[11]R. Lejeune, *Christoph Blumhardt and His Message* (Rifton, N. Y.: Plough, 1963), p. 152.
[12]"Love" in *A Theological Word Book of the Bible*, ed. by Alan Richardson (London: SCM Press, 1950), pp. 131-36.
[13]2 Samuel 1:26.
[14]Wirt and Beckstrom, *Living Quotations for Christians*, nos. 1991, 2982.
[15]Calvin Miller, *The Singer* (Downers Grove, Ill.: Inter-Varsity Press, 1976).
[16]Words by W. C. Martin. Copyright © 1910, Charles H. Gabriel. © Renewed 1938, The Rodeheaver Co.
[17]Jeremiah 6:16.
[18]Ralph W. Sockman, *The Highway of God*, Lyman Beecher Lectures (New York: Macmillan, 1942), pp. 178-79.
[19]John 15:13.
[20]Job 13:15.
[21]Cf. the author's *Afterglow* (Grand Rapids: Zondervan, 1975) and *Freshness of the Spirit* (San Francisco: Harper & Row, 1978).

CHAPTER EIGHT: "Why Is This?"

[1]For Queen Mother Athaliah, see 2 Kings 11:1. For Nebuchadnezzar, see 2 Kings 24-25. For Ptolemy and Antiochus Epiphanes, see Flavius Josephus, *Wars of the Jews*, Book 1, ch. 1. For Absalom and Ahithophel, see 2 Samuel 17.
[2]Psalm 139:22, King James Version.
[3]Charles H. Spurgeon, *The Treasury of David* (New York: Funk & Wagnalls, 1892), 2:304.
[4]Tozer, *The Pursuit of God*, pp. 12-13.
[5]Quebedeaux, *The Worldly Evangelicals*. Note especially ch. 9, "Changing Cultural Attitudes."

[6]Job 23:3, 8-9.
[7]Psalms 18:2, 31, 46; 19:14; 27:5-6; 28:1; 61:2; 95:1.
[8]Matthew 7:24.
[9]1 Corinthians 10:3-4.

CHAPTER NINE: "Taunts"

[1]Psalm 69:7-8, 20.
[2]Matthew 27:43.
[3]"Suffer," in Richardson, *Theological Word Book*, pp. 248-53.
[4]Wirt and Beckstrom, *Living Quotations for Christians*, no. 3138.
[5]Samuel Rutherford, "The Savor of Christ" in *Decision* magazine (October 1964), p. 6. See *Letters of Samuel Rutherford* (London: Oliphant, 1891).
[6]Frank Uttley, *The Supreme Physician* (London: James Clark, n.d.), pp. 5-13.
[7]Matthew 5:10.
[8]John 15:20.
[9]1 Samuel 7:9.
[10]Rowland E. Prothero, *The Psalms in Human Life* (London: John Murray, 1905), p. 187.
[11]Cf. "The Passion of SS. Perpetua and Felicitas," probably edited by Tertullian, in E. C. E. Owen, *Some Authentic Acts of the Early Martyrs*, Eng. tr. (London: Clarendon, 1927).
[12]Prothero, *The Psalms in Human Life*, p. 181.
[13]D. Martyn Lloyd-Jones, *Spiritual Depression: Its Causes and Cure* (Grand Rapids: Eerdmans, 1977), p. 224.

CHAPTER TEN: "Cruelty and Deceit"

[1]*The Cloud of Unknowing* (anonymous, fourteenth century), tr. by Ira Progoff (New York: Dell, 1957), p. 72.
[2]Dag Hammarskjöld, *Markings* (London: Faber, 1972), pp. 10, 86.
[3]Archibald MacLeish, *J. B.* (Boston: Houghton Mifflin, 1958), pp. 12, 153.
[4]Mark Van Doren and Maurice Samuel, *The Book of Praise: Dialogues on the Psalms* (New York: John Day, 1975), p. 112.
[5]Psalm 34:12-13.
[6]Psalm 24:3-4.
[7]Ephesians 6:12.
[8]2 Peter 2:1.
[9]1 Corinthians 10:21.
[10]Revelation 21:8.
[11]Psalm 62:9.
[12]John 16:8.
[13]1 Peter 2:20.
[14]Zechariah 4:6.
[15]1 Samuel 7:10-11; Joshua 10:12-14.

CHAPTER ELEVEN: "The Fortress"

[1]Franz Delitzsch, in *Biblical Commentary on the Psalms*, tr. by Bolton, vol. 7 (Edinburgh: T. & T. Clark, 1893), translates Psalm 43:2 "Thou art God, my fortress." E. W. Hengstenberg, in *Commentary on the Psalms*, tr. Fairbairn and Thomson, vol. 2 (Edinburgh: T. & T. Clark, 1855), has "You are my fortification—God." J. M. Powis Smith, in *The Psalms* (Chicago: University of Chicago Press, 1926), renders it "For thou, O God of my fortress." J. A. Alexander, in *The Psalms Translated and Explained* (New York: Charles Scribner, 1863), says "The word means properly 'my place of strength,' 'my stronghold,' 'my fortress.'"

[2]Herbert Spencer, *First Principles* (London: Williams and Norgate, 1862), ch. 1.

[3]Job 13:24.

[4]Psalm 44:23-24.

[5]Psalm 88:14-18.

[6]Hebrews 12:11.

[7]James 1:2-4, 12.

[8]Francis Bacon, *Essays* (New York: Hurst, 1883). Cf. essay "Of Adversity."

[9]Perry Miller, *New England Mind*, p. 489.

[10]Exodus 3:14; Malachi 3:6; Obadiah 15; Job 38:4.

[11]Isaiah 53:5-6.

[12]Psalm 2:1.

[13]Pitirim A. Sorokin, *Man and Society in Calamity* (New York: E. P. Dutton, 1943), pp. 306, 319.

CHAPTER TWELVE: "The Angel of Light"

[1]Acts 17:27.

[2]Delitzsch, *Biblical Commentary on the Psalms*, 7:61.

[3]Exodus 15:13.

[4]Maclaren, *The Book of Psalms*, 2:53.

[5]Alexander, *The Psalms Translated and Explained*, p. 364.

[6]1 John 2:9-11.

[7]1 John 1:7.

[8]John 3:19-21.

[9]Isaiah 49:6.

[10]Romans 13:9-10, 12.

[11]A. B. Simpson, *Walking in the Spirit* (Harrisburg: Christian Publications, n.d.), p. 95.

[12]Wirt, *Afterglow* and *Freshness of the Spirit*.

[13]1 John 4:7-8, 12-13, 20.

[14]Wirt, *Afterglow*, ch. 12, pp. 53-55.

[15]Mark 3:33, 35.

[16]Luke 10:30-37.

[17]1 John 4:19.

[18]Psalm 118:26.

[19]Matthew 26:39.

CHAPTER THIRTEEN: "The Angel of Truth"

[1]John G. Whittier, "The Eternal Goodness" in *Complete Poetical Works of John Greenleaf Whittier* (Boston: Houghton Mifflin, 1891), p. 442.

[2]John R. W. Stott, *Understanding the Bible* (London: Scripture Union, 1972), p. 184.

[3]Ibid., pp. 190-203 *passim*.

[4]J. Theodore Mueller, "The Holy Spirit in the Scriptures" in *Revelation and the Bible*, ed. by Carl F. H. Henry (Grand Rapids: Baker, 1958), pp. 273-76.

[5]"Climbing on Course," column in *Beyond* magazine (Jungle Aviation and Radio Service, Waxhaw, N.C.), vol. 4, no. 6 (January 1977).

[6]William Butler Yeats, "The Second Coming" in *The Poems of W. B. Yeats*, Variorum ed. (New York: Macmillan, 1957), pp. 401-2.

[7]Robert O. Ferm, "Grasping the Bible's Authority" in *Decision* magazine (February 1964), p. 3.

CHAPTER FOURTEEN: "The Mountain"

[1]Psalm 50:7-11.

[2]1 Kings 8:23, 27-30.

[3]Isaiah 66:1-2; cf. Acts 7:49-50.

[4]Maclaren, *The Book of Psalms*, 2:53.

[5]Ibid.

[6]Psalm 89:1-2.

[7]Robert Louis Stevenson, *The Ebb Tide* (New York: Grosset & Dunlap, 1937), p. 170.

[8]Rabbi William G. Braude, tr., *Midrash on the Psalms* (New Haven: Yale University Press, 1959), p. 445.

[9]Psalm 29:2; 1 Chronicles 16:29, King James Version.

[10]From the song "We Have Come Into His House" by Bruce Ballinger. Copyright © 1976 by Canticle Publications, Inc., Mission, Kansas.

[11]Luke 4:14-22; Matthew 7:21-23; 6:5-7; Mark 11:15-17; 13:2; Matthew 5:23-24.

[12]Psalm 139:7-8, 12.

[13]Brother Lawrence of the Resurrection, *The Practice of the Presence of God*, tr. by Delaney (Garden City, N.Y.: Image Books, 1977), pp. 41-42, 49-50.

CHAPTER FIFTEEN: "The Altar"

[1]The Hebrew word *Shekinah* (not found in the Old Testament) meant literally "dwelling" and signified the glory of God's presence.

[2]Isaiah 61:3.

[3]Song of Songs 2:8; 4:9; 6:3, 2, King James Version.

[4]Odes 3 and 15 in "The Odes of Solomon," edited by J. H. Charlesworth from early texts and published in *Decision* magazine (October 1975), pp.

8-9; also by Oxford University Press. Copyright © 1973 by Oxford University Press.

[5]2 Corinthians 12:2.

[6]Kenneth E. Kirk, *The Vision of God*, Bampton Lectures, abridged (London: Longmans, Green, 1935), p. 145.

[7]Revelation 15:2.

[8]Plato, *The Republic*, tr. by Benjamin Jowett (New York: Modern Library, 1957), pp. 100-108.

[9]Phil Kerr, *Music in Evangelism* (Glendale, Calif.: Gospel Music Publishers, 1950), p. 66.

[10]Ibid., p. 23.

[11]L. T. Remlap, ed., *The Gospel Awakening: Sermons and Addresses of the Great Revival Meetings Conducted by Moody and Sankey* (Chicago: J. Fairbanks, 1879), pp. 763-64.

[12]Luke 5:8.

[13]Thomas à Kempis, *The Imitation of Christ*, book 1, ch. 2, p. 29.

[14]2 Corinthians 6:4, 8-10.

[15]Acts 14:27.

[16]Quoted in John R. MacDuff, *The Hart and the Water-brooks: a Practical Exposition of the Forty-second Psalm* (New York: Robert Carter, 1863), p. 227.

CHAPTER SIXTEEN: "Hope"

[1]Alexander, *The Psalms Translated and Explained*, p. 362; D. Martyn Lloyd-Jones, *Spiritual Depression: Its Causes and Cure*, p. 13.

[2]Ibid.

[3]Spurgeon, *The Treasury of David*, 2:301.

[4]Joseph Parker, *The People's Bible: Discourses Upon Holy Scripture* (London: Funk & Wagnalls, n.d.), 12:204.

[5]In Spurgeon, *The Treasury of David*, 2:313. Taken from Samuel Clarke's *Mirrour*.

[6]Ibid., 2:302.

[7]Alexander, p. 358; Christopher Love (1657 A.D.) in Spurgeon, *The Treasury of David*, 2:311.

[8]Delitzsch, *Biblical Commentary on the Psalms*, 7:57-58.

[9]Sherwood E. Wirt, *Go Tell It and Other Poems* (Kansas City: Beacon Hill, 1979), p. 37.

[10]From William C. Conant, *Narratives of Remarkable Conversions and Revival Incidents* (New York: Derby & Jackson, 1858), pp. 197-98. Reprinted in *Decision* magazine (March 1961), p. 14.

[11]Interview with John Brodie by Don Freeman, courtesy of the *San Diego Union* (25 April 1979).

[12]John 1:29.

[13]John 1:33.

[14]Maclaren, *The Book of Psalms*, 2:53.

[15]Hebrews 11:39-40.
[16]Psalms 30:1; 86:4; 123:1; 143:8.
[17]Isaiah 40:9.
[18]Lamentations 3:40-41.
[19]Luke 21:28.
[20]John 12:32.
[21]James 4:10.
[22]John 3:30, King James Version.
[23]Sir William Gilbert, "My Boy, You May Take It From Me," from the Gilbert and Sullivan operetta *Ruddigore*.
[24]John 4:11.

CHAPTER SEVENTEEN: "Selah"

[1]Tozer, *The Pursuit of God*, p. 17.
[2]Isaiah 44:2-3.
[3]Ezekiel 36:25-27.
[4]Luke 24:49.
[5]Genesis 12:2-3; 15:7; Exodus 33:14; Deuteronomy 18:15-19; Hebrews 9:15; James 2:5; 1 Thessalonians 4:15-18.
[6]Psalm 77:7-8.
[7]Hebrews 11:39-40.
[8]Luke 11:13; 24:49.
[9]Acts 1:4; 2:33, paraphrased; 2:38-39.
[10]Galatians 3:14.
[11]Ephesians 1:13, paraphrased.
[12]Hebrews 10:36.
[13]John 7:39, King James Version.
[14]Psalm 139:6.
[15]John Oxenham's poem "A High Way and a Low" is found in *1000 Quotable Poems*, ed. by T. C. Clark (Chicago: Willett, Clark, 1937), p. 7.
[16]Sir William Gilbert, "I Have a Song to Sing, O" from the Gilbert and Sullivan operetta *The Yeomen of the Guard*.
[17]Romans 15:30.
[18]Psalm 133:1.
[19]Ephesians 5:18.
[20]Harold J. Ockenga, "The Third He," in *Decision* magazine (January 1969), p. 15.
[21]Psalm 124:7.

Index